Secrets OF THE Career Game

Secrets of the Career Game

36 Simple Strategies to Win in the Workplace

KENDALL BERG

HARRIMAN HOUSE LTD
Website: harriman.house

First published in 2025 by Harriman House, an imprint of Pan Macmillan
Associated companies throughout the world
www.panmacmillan.com

Paperback ISBN: 978-1-80409-111-1
eBook ISBN: 978-1-80409-112-8

British Library Cataloguing in Publication Data
A CIP catalogue record for this book can be obtained from the British Library.

Printed and bound in India by Repro India Ltd.

CONTENTS

INTRODUCTION

IMAGINE I TOLD you to sit down and play a game—let's say it looks a bit like chess, but the board and pieces are subtly different. You're sure you've never played this game, but you can tell it's competitive, so when I refuse to tell you the rules and then ask you to stake your livelihood and that of your family on the outcome, how would you respond?

You would probably decline, unwilling to gamble your future on a game you don't understand. You might think, "What person in their right mind would agree to such a thing?" You might even look at me like I was crazy and simply walk away.

And yet, millions of people walk into (or log onto) their workplaces day after day without understanding the rules of the game they are playing—*the career game*—and willingly choose to gamble their futures.

Like ostriches with their heads in the sand, they sit down at their dusty cubicle (or now more commonly open floorplan), set their laptop in their docking station, and prepare for an endless drone of virtual meetings. Or they walk into the warehouse, music blaring to drown out the sounds of supply chain optimization, and get to work stocking boxes in a never-ending cycle of procurement and fulfillment.

These are only examples of a situation found across all industries: The vast majority of employees work hard, delivering on all the requirements of their core job with little to no recognition from their leadership, all the while hoping for a 2–3% raise at year end and a "job well done." Meanwhile, they watch their counterparts gab at the happy hour, deliver mediocre work, and ascend to the highest levels of leadership at three times the speed.

So, what is the key to success in the career game? It is understanding that while the work that you do is important, everything else you are *not* doing is just as important, if not more so. It is learning the right way to position yourself for opportunities, relationships, and promotions regardless of the type of work that you do. Most importantly, it is to stop gambling, learn the rules of the game, and start playing to win.

At some point during our transition to adulthood, we stop asking ourselves "What do I want to be when I grow up?" and start thinking "I should have it all figured out by now, right?" The reality is that in very few cases do we enter adulthood really knowing what we want to be when we "grow up." We have moved away from the dreams and aspirations of passion-filled careers toward steady, dependable, repetitive jobs that pay the bills.

We were brought up to believe that the best way to be successful and earn an income was to pack up and work for someone else day after day, gradually increasing our value as we ascend through the workplace hierarchy.

But so many of us have since found that without rapid progression and the ability to exert our influence, we quickly stagnate, and in more cases than not, burn out.

Over the course of my time as an executive and career coach, I have encountered thousands of people who are frustrated, overwhelmed, and uninformed. They were promised a career that was fulfilling and challenging, as well as an employer who cared about them and their progression as an individual. What they received instead was a job they go to each day, repeating the same exhausting work, for a boss that is not invested—if they are even available.

Gone are the days of taking good care of an employee through a comprehensive system of onboarding, training, and pension plans; now workers face the sad reality of "sink or swim" environments, competency evaluations, and 9-Boxes. Especially in the wake of the

Covid-19 pandemic, countless employees are waking up to the reality of their futures and questioning their career paths. They are looking around their workplace at people in the same boat and wondering, "Is this really all there is?"

I work with these dispirited individuals to help them understand what is happening behind the closed doors of senior leadership and how they can transform themselves into the business savants and leaders that they want to be. This work has led to me being featured in publications such as *Newsweek* and *Business Insider*, and some of the top executives in Fortune 500 companies around the world seek me out for career advice. It has shown me that many of the lessons that I took for granted in my own career are not widely taught. When playing without having learned these lessons, the career game will be fraught with missteps, slowness, and lack of clarity.

I was offered a CFO position before I was 30, managed diverse teams for some of the largest global financial services institutions, and built up a network comprising some of the most influential C-suite leaders in the world. I was often requested to work on the most impactful projects in my organization, lead large-scale transformation projects, and mentor more junior team members with aspirations of climbing the career ladder quickly. How did I achieve these things? I understood the game I was playing. I ensured that I interacted with the various players for maximum value to my career, and I can teach you how to do exactly that.

There's one crucial rule that's common to both chess and the career game: Even when you start off as a pawn, it's possible to become the queen—the most valuable piece on the board. To do that, you must learn how to identify the tasks that will add maximum value to your career, how to understand the vernacular of leadership, and how to navigate interpersonal conflict successfully. Once you've mastered these elements, you'll find yourself in the right position for queening.

The problem is, figuring this all out on your own requires having supportive leadership and mentors, access to conversations that often occur at the highest levels of management, and an abundance of time that, quite candidly, you don't have.

But don't be disheartened. I was once told that you should put twice as much work into improving yourself as you do anything else. If you choose to invest in yourself first, you will ultimately find the success you want rather than the stagnation, frustration, and inaction that have led to you picking up this book in the first place. So here's the good news: If you're willing to invest time, effort, and work into yourself, I can teach you how to get recognition for the good work that you do and accelerate your career. You need only keep reading.

Ready to get started? Let's go…

CHAPTER 1
What is the Game?

mer·i·toc·ra·cy

/merətäkrəsē/ noun: meritocracy

The holding of power by people selected on the basis of their ability.

THE CAREER GAME is laden with so many cleverly hidden and unspoken rules that *most* employees don't know how to play it. While individuals may be hired to complete the tasks listed on an ambiguous job description, their ability to successfully perform in that role and excel beyond it is highly dependent on their soft skills and their adherence to internal company rules, many of which are never spoken aloud. This means that progression in your career is rarely based on merit or your ability to deliver technical tasks, it is instead a hybrid assessment of your ability to build strong relationships, navigate workplace culture, and advocate for yourself.

To understand the core rules of the game, let's address the primary problem most individuals face: I am working hard, often overtime hours, but I am not getting promoted. How could this be possible? So often, many of us believe in quantity over quality. We dedicate hours of overtime to work that we perceive to be important, regardless of priority or impact level. We do this because we believe that our benevolent leaders will see our efforts and reward us.

The reality of the workplace is that little to none of this belief is valid. While you may get lucky with a good leader who rewards hard work every once in a while, or overtime efforts that do add value and drive things forward, more often than not this approach to work will not help you achieve your goals.

We need to move away from thinking of ourselves in terms of our basic workplace functions—as order-takers, widget-producers, and output-machines—and understand that we are individuals who add unique value to the system and ultimately meet our clients' needs. Our work exists to serve others. We work to add value, apply our skills, and give of our personal gifts in a way that will help others achieve *their* personal goals or the goals of their organization. This mindset means that we should think of our boss, leaders, and company as our key clients; receiving the skills and value that we provide.

This mindset is crucial to unlocking the first secret of the career game:

Secret #1: You are an entrepreneur, and your career is your business

Imagine you run your own business, where your skills and abilities are in high demand. Where everything you do garners the attention and accolades of the client, with you delivering a superior product that continues to drive demand even higher. You would likely start to charge more for your services and expand your prospect net in order to serve more people and drive more income. Now put your career in place of that business. As you build up your skills and the value you can offer to your leadership team, and in turn to your company, you will expand your network to include more people to whom you may one day add value—while charging more for your services.

This progression in your career will allow you to move up the chain into more senior positions, maintain a high level of demand for your skills, and ensure you are spending your time in the appropriate places; adding value to your clients and building out your network to include potential future clients.

Run your career like a business

You cannot be in high demand if you jump to meet every request from your client without evaluating its priority. You would not ask your air conditioning installer to fix your dishwasher (because they specialize in a specific skill), or expect a laundromat to prioritize washing your one shirt over the 50 items that had come into the shop before yours (because it is not a higher priority).

The same should be true in your career. You cannot expect yourself to be able to do all things for all people or to jump at the most recent request rather than completing the highest priority tasks. When you start to see yourself as a product of your business, you can begin to deliver stronger and more valuable impact to your company, rather than becoming an order-taker without clear prioritization or direction. Then, as you hone your skills and establish your personal brand (more about this in Chapter 4), you will expand your network to include the biggest influencers inside your company—as well as potential new employers.

This expansion of your network with influential stakeholders will allow you to find long-term success in your career. But it's not always easy. Let's look at Erin, a client of mine, who struggled with this concept of 'expanding her business.' Erin worked for a large company and was constantly going above and beyond. She worked 80–100-hour weeks regularly, often took work home at night, and was always focused on delivering business requirements. When individuals in partner groups dropped the ball regarding her initiatives, she swooped in, picking up the pieces to deliver on timelines and ensure leadership was none the wiser. She sounds like a star employee, right?

Unfortunately, Erin struggled to build her internal network.

When she had first joined the firm, she caused some tension with a key stakeholder called Bob regarding the strategic direction of their work. They had some vehement arguments and silent standoffs that set a negative tone for their relationship. Rather than focusing on repairing their relationship and finding common ground, the two decided avoidance was an easier path.

Their relationship continued to be strained and eventually ended with Bob hiring someone in his own team to do Erin's job. This would ensure that Bob and Erin never had to interact, and he would be able to push his preferred strategy internally. Erin would be refocused on a different area of the business under a different leader and share resources with this newly appointed counterpart.

At this point I'll let you guess whether Erin got promoted. The answer is no. Though Erin was a great employee on paper, always delivering on her core job requirements and even going above and beyond for the company, ultimately this damaged stakeholder relationship held her back and eventually caused her to switch companies. In a straight meritocracy, Erin would have been considered a rock star and Bob's opinion of her wouldn't have mattered at all, but that is not the reality that we all live and work in.

Don't be like Erin. Instead, identify influential stakeholders who might impact your career progression and work with them rather than against them where you can.

This teaches us the second secret of the game:

Secret #2: Relationships matter more than the work

The work is important. You cannot be successful in your career if you do not understand how to do your job, but the reality is that good relationships can overshadow bad work. The reverse is never true. No matter how great you are at your job, if people don't want to work with you, you will stagnate and often find yourself managed out. Think back to the business analogy and suppose you fixed roofs.

It wouldn't matter if you fixed roofs better than anyone else in the world if you never responded to people's calls, argued with them regarding the best approach or color, or belittled their questions and ideas. Eventually, word would spread that you ran a bad business and were difficult to work with, ending the demand and soon closing you down. The same is true in your career. If you cannot find ways to build strong relationships with your clients and stakeholders, you will ultimately fail.

Develop your work relationships

This requires intention, time, and good communication (especially if you work remotely). You must seek individuals out not just for work-related requests, but also simply to learn more about them as people and understand how their skills and work complement your own. Building these relationships will set you up for success later and prevent career stagnation.

If you attend work in-person, so are in physical proximity of your coworkers and leaders, this includes taking them out for coffee or lunch, attending happy hours and teambuilding events, and scheduling quarterly 30-minute meetings to touch base with the most influential people in your organization. While building these relationships can feel easier in an on-site job, this strategy is applicable in any environment if you are intentional with your time and resources. Use your available tools to schedule virtual coffee chats and touch base, reserving time on people's calendars to create deeper relationships and bonds. Then—and this is essential—document what you learn and follow through by referencing it on future calls and engagements: make a note of your boss's daughter's name and ask how she's doing at nursery on your next call; jot down any hints at hobbies and pastimes senior leaders mention and later ask whether they've had any spare time to enjoy them. Perhaps even develop a passing knowledge of those hobbies!

This is a good time to share a story about a peer of mine, Stacy, one of the most knowledgeable people I have ever worked with. She not only knew how to perform her job, she understood every potential roadblock or issue that she could face and had an attention to detail unmatched by anyone I've met. There was just one problem: I hated working with her (and I wasn't alone).

While Stacy was undoubtably the subject matter expert (or SME) in her particular field, and was revered for her knowledge by hundreds of my peers, she was unbelievably difficult to work with. She would refuse to share her knowledge; would hoard tasks, refusing to delegate to the people on her team; and would even use strong, if not abrasive, language when discussing changes or improvements for the organization. She was so concerned that she would lose her job if other people understood what she did, that she chose to ensure that her knowledge could never be duplicated in the hope that she could never be fired.

I sat in on her competency review (we'll discuss these more in Chapter 5) about six months after I started working with her. To set the stage, all of the leaders in our organization sat in a closed room discussing individuals who were eligible for promotion and assessing year-end ratings across our division. There were hundreds of names on the board, and imagine my surprise when I saw that Stacy was listed under the promotion candidates. I couldn't believe it. Was she knowledgeable? Absolutely. Was she ready to manage a team? Absolutely not.

Stacy's manager made his case for her promotion, extolling her many technical accomplishments of the previous year and her necessity to the organization. Heads around the room nodded in agreement. Voices chimed in to mention other projects she had led and the sheer volume of work she had completed. In a true meritocracy this would have been enough, but someone raised their hand.

Their question silenced the room: "Does anyone actually like working with her?"

Now, before you decide that the speaker was the worst person in that room, honestly ask yourself: Would you want to work for someone who refused to train you, wouldn't delegate their work, and would verbally berate you if you did something wrong? I thought not.

The gathered leaders looked from one to another, silently debating if they wanted to share their negative experiences of Stacy with the room at large. The speaker continued, "My team will actively avoid working with her if they can, through fear of her communication style. Do we feel she has the soft skills needed to lead a team?" Their question was genuine. Perhaps others' experience with Stacy has been completely different.

Unfortunately for Stacy, the issue was common to many individuals in the room. Slowly others started speaking out about difficult situations they had faced with her. In that one meeting, Stacy's status dropped from potential promotion candidate to someone known to need improvement at her current level.

So make sure you make the conscious effort to learn about and understand the people you'll be working with, on both a professional and personal level. When you do, the chances are you'll get along much better in both capacities and build advocates rather than adversaries.

This leads us to the third secret of the game:

Secret #3: Communication is key

How you communicate complexity, difficulty, and risks over the course of your career directly correlates to your long-term success. It's not just *what* you communicate, but *how* you communicate, that matters. If you cannot stay calm in difficult situations and explain your reasoning clearly, you will plateau in middle management (if you make it that far). If you cannot disagree effectively, share your opinions clearly, and articulate your value consistently you will end up stuck (or fired).

The worst feedback I ever received in my career was, "You are great at your job, but you aren't great to work with." (Yes, at one point I was a Stacy). The best compliment I ever received in my career was, eight years later: "I aspire to communicate as well as you do in difficult situations." Quite the turnaround. I am living proof that every rule in the game can be learned, and every skill can be taught if you are willing to spend the time and effort required to improve. This turnabout in my career is what led to me eventually becoming a career coach and sharing these rules with my global audience.

Upskilling my communication has allowed me to build a robust network of executives and leaders at various companies across the country, as well as establish my own brand and reputation, ultimately manifesting in this book. It helped me progress through the ranks of leadership in companies I worked for quickly and deliver value more effectively. It also helped me highlight my own skills and articulate my impact more broadly.

Upskill your communication

Whether you're an introvert or an extrovert, neurotypical or neurodivergent, outgoing or reserved, you can (and frankly must) learn to communicate well. This ability to convey your perspective to the many differing personality types you'll encounter in the workplace will be the biggest contributor to your overall growth and progression. It will also allow you to better summarize your accomplishments in order to find new opportunities in the future. As you build out your specialty, you can seek out new and better ways to apply your communication skillset, both within your company and externally.

There are many aspects to communication that we will cover over the course of this book that are meant to help you elevate your manner of interacting with others, but understanding the goal behind communication is the first step. Most people mistake communication in the workplace as defense. They assume that the purpose of sharing your work, your value, your needs, or your recommendations is to defend your own opinion and perspective. That by swaying your audience to your side, you'll be able to convince them of your importance and your value.

But what you are really doing is communicating to your audience the impact of your work in terms of *their* work, values, and needs. If you can understand what your audience cares about (their biggest pain points, their highest priorities, and their loftiest goals) you can tailor your story to their wants and needs and be far more effective. Do this before your meetings by writing a list of your attendees and what you think their biggest priorities are. Then jot down two or three metrics or facts you have that are relevant to each attendee's priority and your topic. Be prepared to speak to those points and relate them to each individual by name.

And so, we come to the fourth unspoken secret of the game:

Secret #4: No one is responsible for your career but you

If you choose to stay in a toxic workplace, or in a team that doesn't value your skills and contributions, the only person who gets hurt is you.

If you take the first job offer that you get every time you are searching, regardless of how it matches your passions, skills, or values, the only person who gets held back is you.

If you stay loyal to a company that doesn't promote you or give you opportunities for growth, the only person who ends up stuck is you.

If you continue working for a bad leader without at least attempting to 'manage up' (by which I mean manage your relationship with your manager), the only person who struggles is you. Do not give anyone (the best boss or the worst boss) control over your career. In the end, only you can decide how quickly you grow and advance.

Accept responsibility for your career

When you take responsibility for your own career, and you refuse to give others the power to limit your growth and development, you will start to see exponential progression. But this does not mean you can do everything on your own. If you reflect on Secret#2: *Relationships matter more than the work*, you will see that we need others to help us hone our skills, develop ourselves, and find opportunities for progression. In other words, you need a network.

Your network is key for finding upward progression within your company as well as sourcing a new role when you find yourself in a bad fit.

Think of your job like dating and trying to find a life partner. Your resume is a dating profile geared towards appealing to your ideal mate, and interviews are a bit like speed dating, hoping you find out enough in a short time period to determine a match. Getting the job is a bit like going steady to decide if marriage is on the cards for you both. If you ignore the red flags from a company, you will end up in an unhealthy 'marriage.' If you have clear expectations of the companies you work for and the roles you take, you have a higher probability of landing the right 'life partner.'

When you are in interviews, you should use your questions at the end of each interview to determine if the role and the company have the values and opportunities that you need. The best way to do this is to write out three 'passion statements' describing what fills your cup at work (excluding tasks). Here are my examples:

- "I am passionate about having a broad scope of influence and being able to work on different tasks each day."
- "I am passionate about leading and developing a team—creating the next generation of leaders."
- "I need to see the output of my efforts directly—as a result I like working on internally facing teams, rather than externally, for a medium-sized organization."

Questions I might ask in an interview that tie to these passions would be:

- "What does a standard day look like in this role?"

- "How often are new projects or scopes of work assigned?"
- "What is the team size that I will be responsible for coaching?"
- "What does progression and growth within the team look like for these individuals?"
- "How do we measure success in this role?"
- "How do I ensure that my internal stakeholders feel that they are getting what they need?"

The answers to these questions will give me a much better idea of how this role will align to my passions and whether there will be a long-term future for me with the team.

You should also be asking about specific culture requirements you have from the company. Examples of this could include:

- "How does the company support diversity and inclusion?"
- "Does the company offer mentorship, and if so is this arranged formally or informally?"
- "Are there culture or community groups that I can join related to [X] interest?"

Once you have answers to all of your questions you should feel much more prepared to evaluate the role as a potential fit. If you are still unsure, there are two more pieces of advice to follow:

- First, if the hiring manager is the person you liked least in the interview process, don't take the job. Your direct manager has more influence over your success and progression than almost anyone else in the company.
- Second, if you cannot tell whether or not the company culture is genuine, ask to speak to peers on the team. Generally, companies will allow this and it will give you far more insight into the personalities of the group and what progression looks like from within.

Being intentional and strategic about which roles you take (and which roles you don't) will set you on a better long-term career path. Don't let yourself fall into the trap of an 'accidental career' when you could instead be pursuing your optimal opportunities.

What does all of this mean? It means that the game is real whether you want to acknowledge it or not, and every company in the world has their own internal politics at play. Learning to successfully navigate this game does not require becoming inauthentic to who you are, pandering to people you don't respect, or overhauling your personality to fit some absurd corporate mold, ***but*** it does require understanding the rules of the game and making strategic and wise choices when it comes to your career.

An individual in a job that aligns with their skills, passions, and interests will always be more successful than someone who ends up at odds with the role or the company culture. The first step in finding that successful alignment is understanding the type of work that will allow you to leverage your unique skills and make an impact on your company—let's get into that next.

CHAPTER 2

Promotable and Non-Promotable Tasks

pro•mote

/prəmōt/ verb: promote

Advance or raise (someone) to a higher position or rank.

HERE'S A FACT that they don't teach us in school: Some of the best work that you do won't help get you promoted. We are taught that good work returns good grades, and bad work will get you a failing grade or worse: expelled. But in the workplace, not all work is created equal (a bit like how homework doesn't contribute directly to your exam grades).

So how can we separate work that *will* help us get promoted from that which *won't*? We can start by dividing work into the following broad categories:

1. Work that is core to the maintenance of your position; we will refer to this as "business as usual" (or BAU) work.

2. Work that drives forward the goals of the organization and generally will include collaboration across various groups; we will refer to this as high-impact or high-visibility work,
3. Work that makes you more marketable or valuable as an individual through the development of your personal skills or improves culture and engagement across your organization; we will refer to this as self-development or engagement work

Note that some work may start as BAU but evolve into high-impact work if you apply the right skills and intention.

When you begin your career, much of your job is BAU work. You prove your abilities and acumen through the accurate and on-time delivery of these tasks. Then as you progress and show your competence, your manager will, ideally, start to give you more complicated, large-scale tasks so that you can continue to develop and build new skills, which will then help you further your career. However, when you work for a poor leader who does not give you these opportunities, or when you struggle to show your ability to do well in your role, you will find yourself without these stretch opportunities and starting to stagnate.

If I were to hire someone to run a report every Thursday at 8am and send it to a distribution list of five stakeholders, and the person I hired did so with no mistakes, but never contributed anything else to the team or the organization, would they deserve a promotion? The answer is a resounding no.

What if I hired them to run the report, they did so beautifully, but they never showed me the report and I never heard about it from the relevant stakeholders? Would they get promoted? No, and perhaps they would even get fired—despite completing their core job—because no one was aware of the work they were doing or its value.

What if they never ran the report? They just sat at their desk all day on TikTok and never contributed. Would they get promoted? No. They would get fired (after six months of deliberation and documentation with HR, but that is an issue for another day).

What if they automated the report during their first week and turned their focus to understanding the key problems of those five stakeholders, then created an expanded dashboard built off the report to solve those problems and led an operationalization initiative to have the solutions ingrained in their respective divisions? Let's say they also established key performance indicators (KPIs) to measure the success of those divisions based on the data and used it to prepare an executive summary of the dashboard's impact. Would they get promoted? Damn right they would!

All four of these scenarios start with the same person, the same job requirements, and the same measurements for success—yet one leads my employee to plateau, two see her get fired, and only in one is she promoted. So what is the key difference between them?

It's the balance of two equally powerful forces: intention and opportunity. We need to intentionally seek out ways to apply our unique skills and evolve our work for the betterment of our organization, and we need to identify the best opportunities to add value to the company and our leadership.

How do we determine the best ways to avoid or enhance non-promotable tasks so that we can focus on higher-impact work?

First, we must understand how to recognize non-promotable tasks in order to determine how we can best approach work we are assigned over the course of our careers.

I define BAU as the following:

- All of the tasks that are core to your job,
- Any work isolated to your direct team,
- Repeatable, trainable tasks (anything with a standard operating procedure or SOP),
- Anything that could be automated.

Now don't panic—*you should have some BAU* as part of your job, no matter your seniority. Even if you now realize that *everything* you do is BAU, stay with me. I have a plan. It is also critical to mention that if you are in a highly technical role (a scientist, engineer, or software developer, for example) you will have a significantly higher percentage of BAU work than people in many other roles. Not *all* BAU is non-promotable, but most of it is—unless you can develop it into an impactful opportunity (like my employee did in the fourth recent example).

Let's look at another example—this one from the real world. Meet Alex. Alex had a very technical role and was great at BAU. She worked a lot of overtime fielding requests from peers, leaders, and other departments to make up for a lack of technical skills elsewhere in her organization. She worked for a good boss who ultimately had her best interests in mind, but she wasn't informing him of the dozens of requests she received daily or the 20–30 hours of overtime she was working each month.

While Alex's superiors saw her working to improve her soft skills, she was behind the scenes responding to five times the requests of her closest peer. She was a powerhouse of productivity, production, and output; but struggled to communicate that level of effort effectively. Not to mention that she was rarely given credit or acknowledgment for her efforts by the stakeholders she helped. She was simply a means to an end to most of them; they needed data, and she could deliver.

When Alex first came to me for career advice, she was working near-constant overtime, burning herself out, and yet was still not being promoted. This led to frustration and stagnation, which also held her back.

Do you identify with Alex? Hers is a common problem. It leads to burnout as we quickly fill our days with small, mundane requests out of lack of prioritization or direction. Many of my clients are a lot like Alex, and hers is a problem common to all industries, jobs, and even seniority levels. A few lucky sufferers manage to get ahead regardless—if their boss is paying close attention and sees their efforts—but they generally fail to jump to more senior levels.

Rather than hoping we're among the lucky ones, let's look at how to ensure we aren't overwhelmed by BAU.

Secret #5: You must have and maintain healthy boundaries

I don't want you to work *more.* I won't even encourage you to work *harder.* Instead I want to teach you how to structure your time and efforts effectively to achieve your goals. This starts with setting boundaries. No matter how long you have been with a company, or what title you hold, you must figure out your boundaries. They could be:

- No work on the weekends.
- No work after 5pm.
- You will always take at least 30 minutes for lunch.
- No work when you or your family is sick.
- No responding to emails after 6pm.
- You will always leave work when your kids or spouse have important events.
- You will not take on additional projects when you are at maximum capacity.

Only you know what your personal boundaries are, but you should write them down, understand their impacts, and be prepared to defend why they are important to you. There may of course be times in your career that require you to exercise some additional flexibility with your boundaries, but these should always be timebound and well communicated. For example, you might agree to stay late this week to meet the big deadline on Friday, but will be back to your normal schedule starting Monday. If you don't set some limitations, you will inevitably slip away from your boundaries.

For me, I generally log off work by 5pm, I don't work weekends, and I don't work when my family is sick. These are the boundaries I set with each manager, at each workplace, and I have never received complaints about them.

That being said, there are many companies and teams that will push your boundaries to the breaking point; most leaders will overload you with work until you tell them you can't take any more… and then they will give you a few extra tasks on top. I've worked with many clients over the years who have struggled in these environments and ultimately been fired or released as a result of maintaining their boundaries (or caved to the demands of their companies at great personal sacrifice until they burnt out and left).

What I have learned is that much of the negative perception regarding boundaries comes down to *how* they are maintained rather than the fact that they exist at all. Establishing and maintaining boundaries does not happen at the point where your boundary is about to break; it happens when you take on work and communicate your capacity to your leadership.

Use boundaries to prioritize, bundle, and rebrand

The trick to progressing while holding strict boundaries is that you have to *deliver* within those boundaries. There's a three-step process to achieving this: prioritize, bundle, and rebrand.

Think back to Alex. Her plate was full with BAU requests, and she hadn't set any boundaries to stop more flooding in. Rather than rejecting all of this work, she could have set boundaries to help her prioritize, bundle, and rebrand. These are the three steps you will apply to all of your BAU work moving forward to ensure that you are optimizing these tasks for impact rather than simply delivery (which changes them from BAU to high-impact outputs).

It's essential to use your boundaries to prioritize the work that is on your plate against the full scope of your work to ensure you are working on the *right* tasks. If your boundaries state that you won't work more than 40 hours a week, but you have 60 hours of work in front of you Monday morning, you need to figure out which 20 hours of work can be jettisoned.

When you are evaluating your priorities, the discussions with your boss and your stakeholders change from "Sure, I'll take that on," to

"I can appreciate that this is a high-priority request. Given the other tasks currently on my plate: A, B, and C, are you comfortable with me deprioritizing C in order to make enough space in my capacity to work on this new request?"

What you should try to avoid as you make this transition is harsh rejections that sound like "No, I can't help with this request as I have too much to do," or "Are you going to pay me extra to deliver this project via overtime?" Both of these responses create a negative reaction in your leadership and are more likely to lead to disciplinary action that goes counter to our objective of progression.

Once you've set your priorities, look at bundling your tasks together. Like the example with the weekly report earlier in this chapter, there are often times that you can bundle tasks either with each other or with automation efforts. If, like Alex, you are getting dozens of data requests each week on various marketing initiatives, you can bundle them together to create a self-service dashboard where your stakeholders can access the information themselves, for example.

Once you bundle your work together, it is time to re-brand it. What was simply a report, is now an automation effort that allows leaders to make data-driven decisions based on an automated dashboard. What was many data requests is now a central repository of marketing data that allows leaders to self-service their needs in real time. What was a monthly deck refresh is now a collaborative effort to deliver executive metrics in a timely manner while driving awareness across the organization.

These steps are most often completed in partnership with your boss, primarily to make sure you have the full context of why the work is important, but also to make sure they recognize and appreciate what you're doing. One of the most eye-opening experiences in my career is related to this process.

A few years ago, a teambuilding event at an obstacle course was planned for a Friday. My entire team was set to attend, and we had been looking forward to it for weeks, until I realized that I had 12 separate projects all due that Friday. The entire week leading up to the event, I worked overtime—tirelessly trying to clear things from my plate, only to be hit with roadblocks, change requests, and last-minute additions. When Friday finally rolled around, I was no closer to clearing the tasks off my plate than I had been on Monday. I knew there was no way I could attend with my group. I was devastated.

This is how my boss at the time found me: crying in an office (not so professional I know), stressed over my project load, and planning to skip one of the biggest team events of the year. He sat me down, handed me a piece of paper, and asked me to write out each item due that day and who it was for. Once I did, he gave me some much-needed context on each piece of work, and we agreed that some of them weren't as urgent as I had thought. Before I knew it, we had crossed out three items that could be reassigned or delegated elsewhere. We then circled two that we agreed I could and should complete before the offsite, and for the rest we agreed a series of dates over the next two weeks for them to be delivered.

When I asked him how it was possible to shift things so dramatically, he told me, "I wish I'd known you were working on so many different tasks. I could have delegated some to other members of the team or pushed back on your behalf. We need to start reviewing your workload once a month so that you don't burn yourself out. I'll send emails to the stakeholders today explaining the situation."

After that incident, I set a new boundary: I wouldn't agree to deadlines that would conflict with other important life events.

My manager helped me to learn a valuable lesson about boundaries, but at the same time I was shocked by a realization of a completely different kind: I asked myself, how could he not have known I was doing all of this work? And why was I working on things he deemed unimportant?

The answers taught me one of the most important lessons of my career:

Secret #6: Your boss does not know what you are working on

Full stop. Even if your boss is amazing (which clearly mine at the time was) they simply do not have the time or the inclination to track all of your tasks. It is your responsibility to keep your boss informed regarding your workload and bandwidth. Otherwise, you will end up overloaded, underappreciated, and ready to have a breakdown in a conference room (trust me, I know from experience).

Don't keep your successes secret from your boss

I see it all the time: Individuals who are working hard on a million different projects, increasing their mental load and stress levels exponentially, only for their leadership to be blissfully unaware. Instead, ensure that you have the right communication strategy in place to inform, escalate, and advocate.

You should be meeting one-on-one with your boss at least biweekly (if not weekly). If you aren't having these touchpoints, schedule them right now. Put down this book, open your calendar, and get some time with your boss. If you *are* having them, great! Let's make sure you are using that time purposefully and intentionally.

In a 30-minute one-on-one you should spend ten minutes getting them up to speed on the work that you are doing (inform), while focusing on the impacts. The biggest mistake that I see here is individuals giving a laundry list of tasks to their boss to defend their busy-ness. Instead, you should articulate the value of the work you are delivering in terms of impact (how your work increases revenue, drives efficiency, decreases risk, etc.) and follow with the efforts you are putting forward to support that impact. Feel free to throw in stakeholder names and to look ahead to future deliverables that they should know will impact your capacity as well.

The next ten minutes are for escalations. Just as we don't want to keep the great work you are doing secret from your boss, we don't want to hide potential risks and roadblocks from them until things are on fire—at that point it will be too late. So deliver your escalations and decision points to your boss in tandem with your impact updates. That way they are clear on what you need from them in order to deliver your work effectively.

Lastly, spend the final ten minutes gaining alignment on priorities, discussing any capacity constraints that are risks to your boundaries, and soliciting feedback on your performance and workload (advocate). This will ensure you and your boss are in sync and avoid potential pitfalls like I experienced in the previous example. It also gives you the chance to get feedback and create proactive plans to improve on shortfalls in order to continue your progression. While we will discuss how to do this on a deeper level later in the book, it is important that this is a frequent touchpoint with your boss.

Outside of these structured conversations, you can loop them in on new requests, changes, and escalations as they occur through their preferred method of communication (generally I will CC my boss on emails related to high-profile projects or notoriously difficult coworkers for their awareness). This ensures they stay up to date with what is happening and protects you (in writing) from bad bosses who may seek to undermine your efforts.

What we want to avoid in this strategy is focusing too much on the details of your day to day. Instead, take a holistic view of your scope and impact. This leads us to Secret #7:

Secret #7: How you talk about your work matters

The way people describe their work, skills, and impacts determines people's perception of them and their relative value in the workplace. Rather than describing the work as "running the weekly report" it can be phrased as "enabling data-driven decision-making." This shift in how the work is described changes its meaning, and therefore its importance, to your leadership. Where most people struggle is how to describe a task in terms of its impact. The easiest way I have found to do this is to avoid focusing on what *you* have done in favor of focusing on what *could not* have happened without you.

A project manager, for example, could say that they babysat stakeholders to get information by deadlines, tracked budgetary spend, and created project documentation. Or they could say that they delivered a streamlined solution for technical delivery, increasing development efficiency by 20%, by collaborating with key stakeholders, driving clarity on business requirements, and influencing the business towards the most optimal solution within budget. The latter example is focused on what *wouldn't* have happened without them—the project output— rather than what tasks they completed; then it is supplemented with what *effort* they put into that delivery. This articulates impact and effort much better than a list of their tasks.

Understand the three types of work

Assuming you have identified the BAU work in your job, transformed as much as possible into high-impact efforts, and established your boundaries, what do you focus on next? The two other types of work: high impact/high visibility and self-development/engagement. These types of work are what will really drive your career forward and help you climb the career ladder, so these are what you want to emphasize when it comes to discussing your work.

High-impact/high-visibility work

High-impact/high-visibility work and projects have a few criteria to qualify:

- They drive the company and strategy forward.
- They involve three or more teams/key stakeholders.
- The work aligns with your key skills (we will cover this more in Chapter 3).

- It will solve a key problem or drive impact across the organization.
- The outcome can be measured.

To end up on high-impact/high-visibility projects, you either need leadership to advocate for you, advanced knowledge that the project is happening (so that you can advocate to work on it), or to have come up with the idea yourself. We will cover the first two options later in the book, so let's focus on the third option: The best way to end up on a high-profile project is for it to have been your idea in the first place. Listen to the talk around the watercooler, identify your own complaints and issues around the organization, and make a plan to solve them.

Take Brian, for example: Brian had a great reputation across his entire team and beyond for being a problem-solver. Leadership tapped Brian when there was a big project that needed innovation, organization, and, above all, results. But, surprisingly, Brian's biggest achievement wasn't that big at all.

Early on in his role, after listening to peers, leaders, and clients complain about his company's inconsistent branding at multiple forums, Brian devised a plan. He would work with the creative team to create standard slides and templates for use across the company; everyone from the CEO to the intern would create presentations that looked and felt the same.

This is not a revolutionary idea; it's not even very complex, but it was an idea that no one else at his company had come up with. By simply listening to the people around him and devising a solution, he was able to redirect the branding and cohesiveness of his entire company, driving improved employee experience, client retention, and brand awareness. He was applauded for thinking outside of the box and delivering value to his company with minimal effort. It got him promoted.

When you look at the specific work delivered within the project, it could all be construed as BAU; delivering slides was part of Brian's core job and therefore not a high-visibility activity. But he had an idea that would allow him to drive greater impact across his company, brand himself as an innovator and problem-solver, and solve multiple stakeholders' complaints at once. This is both a transformation of a BAU task as well as a unique idea for an impactful project.

If you are feeling stuck coming up with new ideas to drive value, focus close to home (what are you doing that could be better) and on what people around you are complaining about. Both are treasure troves for new ideas and new impact.

Assuming you work in a utopian business where there are no issues (unlikely), or you are struggling to get backing/support for your ideas (more likely), or you simply have additional bandwidth, you may also have the chance to focus on self-development/engagement work.

Self-development/engagement work

Self-development work must meet a few criteria to be useful to your career progression:

- Your leadership *must* know that the work is taking place (don't undertake training/read books/get coaching without your boss knowing about your investment in yourself).
- It must enhance an already-existing skill that you have (soft skills or technical).
- *Or* it must teach you a new skill that is necessary for your success (communication or technical tools).

Engagement projects also have a few criteria to qualify:

- They must bring diverse groups of people together.
- The efforts must improve/create culture across your organization.
- They must be valuable to both your peers *and* your leadership.

I love building strong team cultures. It is honestly in my top three passions at work and something I strive to do in every role that I hold.

Every person has the ability to influence the culture and engagement of their direct group. You do this either by leading by example or creating programs and infrastructure to allow the group to develop culture together.

Leading by example is where self-development work comes into play. Get a coach or a mentor, sign up for a certification, read more books like this one, listen to podcasts, or undertake training. Use that time to enhance your own skills and deliver more effectively at your job while communicating to your leadership and peers the work—and the value of that work—that you are putting into your own development. Not only will it show leadership that you have potential for growth and investment, it will also inspire those around you to do the same for their own careers and growth.

The second option, creating infrastructure and programs to drive culture, can greatly enhance your team's engagement and show initiative to your leaders. This is something my colleague Jaime understood, and she was able to utilize this type of work to propel her career forward. Jaime knew that while the work was important, how you felt about that work and your coworkers was equally, if not more, important. She proposed and developed a brilliant program called 'Sharp Tank' that rolled out across our firm. I bet you can guess where this is going.

Jaime's program enabled company employees to submit their ideas for new projects. The finance and project management teams would then help them to create a business case, which the employee would present to the company executives. If their project was chosen, they would get the opportunity to implement their idea in the following fiscal year. It was obviously inspired by a popular TV show, but this genius idea drove an absolutely incredible amount of excitement across our company.

Now, if you're a project manager or already a leader, this may not sound too appealing; but imagine how this idea felt to call center employees, engineers, developers, and frontline associates. Suddenly they had an opportunity to do something completely different with their career, if they could come up with a great idea. It sparked innovation, collaboration, and initiative across the company with minimal cost or risk. Jaime's engagement project landed her facetime with the executive team, a huge bonus, and a promotion.

This is proof that engagement work is just as important as your core job tasks. Jaime's job was not to create programs for the firm. It was to deliver on a very specific subset of business requirements in her space, but she had a great idea and the ability to carry it through to completion. You can do the same thing.

Homework assignment #1

It's time for your first homework assignment. Track everything you do over the course of the next week and try to tag it as BAU, high-impact/high-visibility, or self-development/engagement work. Then estimate the percentage of work time you spend on each category. Ideally you should be at 40% BAU, 40–50% high-impact/high-visibility ('impact' for short), and 10–20% self-development/engagement (highly technical roles may shift 10–20% towards BAU and still be considered on track). This will give you a strong baseline on which to build your future efforts.

If you find yourself with too much BAU relative to the rest of your workload, revisit my earlier tips above and prioritize, bundle, and rebrand as much as possible. If that BAU is related to the technical aspect of your role and unable to be re-prioritized, then rebranding is the simplest of these efforts. You should also look at your BAU tasks and tie them directly to a company impact (cost reduction, efficiency gain, revenue increase, etc.). Any tasks that you identify have zero impact need to be re-evaluated with your boss to ensure they are still a good use of your time.

Then move onto impact work. If your percentage of impact work is low, recommend new ideas and innovations, bundle BAU tasks together and rebrand, or volunteer to be on new, exciting projects that may stretch your abilities. A lot of impact work comes down to assertiveness (asking for what you want) and initiative (making recommendations or being intentional about your time). Once you start focusing in this area, you will start to see the BAU naturally decrease.

Lastly, and this is possibly the most important thing I will say in this entire book, invest in yourself. Spend time building up your strongest skills through self-development and engagement work. Understand your value and how to make it shine in the context of your work. Do not sit back, wait to be recognized, and hope for the best. Instead, proactively identify your skills and start influencing your team—activities we will cover in the next chapter.

CHAPTER 3

Your Most Marketable Skills

Skill

/skil/ noun: Skill

The ability to do something well.

HOW WELL DO you know yourself? Most people like to believe that they know themselves well, but in my experience when asked to truly assess themselves, without ego, people generally struggle.

What do I like? What am I good at? How do I add value? These seemingly innocuous questions throw even the most experienced professionals into a tailspin. But, if you intend to lead a fulfilled and successful life, understanding yourself is key.

Knowing yourself, your uniqueness, and your capabilities, sets you up for success when navigating the workplace as well as the career lattice (a term we'll unpack later). Most of us look around at our peers, managers, and coworkers and think to ourselves, "I could do their job. It doesn't look that hard." But while we may have faith in our own capabilities, it is incredibly important to be able to articulate those capabilities, alongside your transferable skills, to your leaders for consistent, and sometimes expedited, progression.

First you must know your advantage. What is it that differentiates you from your peers? Most interviews try to get at the heart of this question, but I see far too many individuals focus instead on what tasks they have completed, what systems they have used, and avoiding negative topics rather than selling potential employers on what makes them different and therefore valuable. To understand your advantage, you must first give up on the notion that you are (or even should be) good at everything.

In many ways, being 'good at everything' is the *worst* thing you can be. As we grow up, schools and education teach us that we need to be passing in every subject. It doesn't matter if your passion is Math or Chemistry, you must do well in English and History as well. This embeds in our psyche a need to be *good*, or at least *average*, in everything that we do. However, studies have shown that business leaders who are good at every skill rate as some of the lowest-performing managers.[1] This is because, without a differentiating factor (or 'spike' as I like to call them), ultimately you will blend into the workforce and appear average rather than extraordinary.

These studies go on to show that having a spike in performance in one or two skills sets you apart drastically from your colleagues and peers, regardless of the weaknesses you may exhibit in other skills. This means that being good at everything is actually worse for your reputation and personal brand than being good at some things and bad at others.

Think back on a leader that you really respected or liked. This can go as far back as primary school or be as recent as a current leader or executive. What about them specifically made you respect them? Odds are they weren't perfect, or even 'good' at everything. But I bet you can pick one or two things that they did exceptionally well. Maybe they were great at communication or had incredible technical proficiency. Maybe they built great teams and cultures, or they were able to innovate new ways of working. They did something better than you and, likely, better than their peers. It set them apart and allowed you to commit them to long-term memory.

This is what you should strive to be. Not good at everything, but instead exceptionally great at *some* things. In order to determine where your exceptional skills (or spikes) may be, try this exercise that I complete with my teams twice a year: Take the following list of 20 skills and attributes and rate yourself on a scale of 1–10 for each. A rating of 10 means that you are better than anyone else at this skill, and 1 should be that you've never displayed that skill before.

1. High integrity/honesty
2. Technical/professional experience
3. Solves problems/analyzes issues
4. Innovates
5. Learning agility/self-development
6. Drives for results
7. Establishes stretch goals
8. Takes initiative
9. Communicates powerfully and prolifically
10. Inspires/motivates others
11. Builds relationships
12. Collaboration and teamwork
13. Strategic
14. Champions change
15. Has customer and external focus
16. Develops others
17. Strong moral character
18. Decision-making
19. Risk-taking
20. Values diversity

Then you will have three other people score you. Ideally this will be your boss, someone who works for you (if applicable) or a respected peer, and a key stakeholder. Once you have all of your scores back, you will average them to get your final scores and then rank them to identify your skill spikes. Spikes tend to be set apart by your other scores by 1–2 points. These will become the area in which you invest most of your time and development; building on a pre-existing spike is more valuable than trying to shore up a weakness, with two exceptions.

- Communicates powerfully and prolifically
- Collaboration and teamwork

If either of these are in your lowest four scores, they *must* be improved. No one can continue to progress their career or scale their growth without being a strong communicator and collaborator. This is why Secret #3 is so important—*communication is key*. Regardless of your industry, job, or seniority level, you *must* be able to communicate effectively.

Once you have identified your spikes, focus on ruthlessly developing them. Find opportunities to highlight your strengths and build them up to be even stronger. My personal spikes are:

- Solves problems/analyzes issues
- Drives for results
- Champions change

Over the course of my career I have utilized these skills to deliver various projects and change initiatives across three industries and five department/organization types (marketing, construction, operations, technology, and data).

For me, the key to building up these spikes has been learning new ways to execute, improving my communication (to better deliver results and champion change), and investing more in myself than in my job (both time and financial investment). I solicit feedback regularly from not just my direct leadership but also stakeholders, peers, and partners on my performance as well as areas for potential improvement across the organization. I have gone through training for various tools and analysis as well as change and project management to better deliver across my spikes for the good of the company.

Once you understand your own personal spikes (and the critical weaknesses that need to be shored up, if you have them) you should develop a plan for how you intend to bolster and grow these strengths. Create 'ceremonies' for feedback and criticism (we will cover this more in Chapter 10), invest in your own development (both time and money), and create a learning plan that will allow you to grow your skills even more. This learning plan can include training, certifications, special projects, mentoring sessions, and more that align with you personally.

You need to stop worrying about your weaknesses and instead focus on the ways you can bolster your own strengths. Look for new projects where your strengths add value, solicit feedback from your stakeholders, and be willing to invest in yourself. This will allow you to have a greater impact on your overall company and thus advocate for more progression.

This is the eighth secret of the game:

Secret #8: If you do not have an impact, you will not see progression

Steve was a very hard worker with high levels of technical acumen. He understood data and how to deliver it in ways I rarely see showcased in the corporate world (more commonly his way of thinking is present in academia), but he did not know how to drive an impact. He had a wonderful reputation across the organization as an asset in his space but was rarely chosen for high-impact projects. When he was moved to my team, it was in order to support a growing focus on data-driven decision-making and opportunities for efficiency improvements, but without clear direction about where he was to fit in the picture.

As I generally do at the start of new projects, I called my team together to throw out ideas. What was going poorly in our organization, where were there bottlenecks, what was going well, and so on. I asked the team to throw out ideas regardless of their probability of being solved, just so that we could better understand what issues we would face.

We were all called together to drive an impact across the organization as a whole, and no idea was to be discounted. I waited patiently as the team ideated and threw out ideas until Steve shared the one idea I had been looking for. It was brilliant. I assigned the project to him with my utmost support.

Although Steve was unused to putting himself out there, with a little encouragement his desire to make an impact surfaced and he then leaned in. He partnered with various stakeholder groups, created a framework and workstreams for execution, and followed through with rapid iteration and testing to deliver results quickly. Then he validated his efforts with various business partners to ensure it would deliver maximum impact to their teams.

This project ended up saving the company millions of dollars and driving more than a 30% efficiency gain. It had tremendous impact on all of our teams and became the internal poster child for new projects and initiatives. For the first time, Steve was no longer the data guy, he was instead an individual who had delivered great impact.

Maximize your impact above all else

It is so much more important to deliver impact than simply to do your job. In Steve's example, we did have a company culture that supported innovation and new ideas as well as a team structure that allowed for a lot of autonomy. Obviously, this is not true at every company, and so you might meet more resistance to—or even flat-out rejection of—new ideas, but even within that resistance there is an opportunity to utilize your skills to drive impact, measure that impact, and then share that impact to your leadership. That is how you will find progression and success.

This is also why it is so important for your spikes identified above to align with the needs of the company you work for. I have not been a star performer at every company I have worked for (shocking, I know). There have been many times where my skills did not align with the needs of my team or company, and I was seen as an average contributor or a cog in the wheel. Despite the fact that my skills and work ethic had not changed, the company in which those skills manifested determined much of my success.

Which brings me to the next secret of the game:

Secret #9: An unneeded skill is unvaluable

If a tree falls in the forest, and no one is around to hear it, does anyone care? A bit of a twist on a more classic saying, but the same applies to your skillset. If you have a skill but no one around you needs it, is it valuable? Generally, the answer will be no. If you think back to my specific spikes (drives for results, solves problems/analyzes issues, and champions change) combined with the fact that I am highly organized and great at time management, I thrive in chaotic environments. The less structure that exists, the better I will shine when I apply my spikes.

I add little to no value in an organization that is highly structured, with very few issues, and has great documentation—because my spikes will add far less impact to the company. Thus, when I search out new opportunities for myself, I am looking for organizations in overhaul, chaos, or general disarray. For many, this type of environment would cause undue anxiety as they struggled to navigate unclear direction, but for me this environment is ideal.

Thinking back on your own personal assessment, what type of environment best fits your skills and interests? Is it a small company or a large company? An organized environment or a chaotic one, for example? Don't worry if you're not sure; I've mapped each skill against the environment they need to be deployed into to maximize their effect.

Skill	Needs of the Company
High Integrity/honesty	Strong company culture and great leaders
Technical/professional experience	Improved business results and employees who invest in new skills
Solves problems/analyzes issues	Improved business results and highly organized processes and teams
Innovates	Strong company culture and automation
Learning agility/self development	Great leaders and employees who invest in new skills
Drives for results	Improved business results and highly organized processes and teams
Establishes stretch goals	Improved business results and increasing revenue
Takes initiative	Great leaders
Communicates powerfully and prolifically	Great leaders and culture of collaboration
Inspires/motivates others	Great leaders
Builds relationships	Great leaders and culture of collaboration
Collaboration and teamwork	Great leaders and culture of collaboration
Strategic	Great leaders and improved business results
Champions change	Highly organized processes and teams
Has customer and external focus	Increasing revenue
Develops others	Leaders
Strong moral character	Great leaders and strong company culture
Decision-making	Great leaders
Risk-taking	Strong company culture and new ideas
Values diversity	Great leaders and strong company culture

Take your strengths where they are most needed

Knowing yourself allows you to identify your strengths, invest in them heavily, and align yourself to roles and companies that will best allow you to shine. Then you can better understand the needs of your key stakeholders and how you deliver value to them.

Assuming both of these exercises are complete, you can assess your current circumstances to evaluate whether or not you are in the right spot. For optimal success and most rapid progression, you must be in a culture that aligns with your strengths. If you have a spike in decision-making but you are in an organization with high levels of bureaucracy, limited autonomy, and incompatible leadership, odds are you are in need of a job change (at a minimum an internal transfer to a department that more closely aligns). If you spike in risk-taking and are working for a venture capitalist firm placing bets on up-and-coming startups, then odds are you are in a strong alignment where your risk-taking spike will be highly valued.

I can give a personal example from my own career where misalignment dramatically stifled me.

I left a highly innovative, startup-like culture, to move to what I call a 'golden ticket' company. We all know these companies; their names alone are enough to propel you to many future opportunities and open doors that would otherwise remain closed. There is likely not a person on the planet that doesn't recognize the names of these companies despite the fact that they may change slightly over time. It would be like asking someone who Michael Jordan was and getting a blank stare—extremely unlikely.

At this point in my career, I had proven out my spikes repeatedly in various companies, roles, and industries. I was excited to 'play with the big guys' in a new role which seemed to have been custom-made for my skills and experience. I turned down a CFO offer at a smaller company to take a VP role that would allow me to make a name for myself and propel my career forward. Big mistake—but we'll soon get to that.

In this large company, rife with bureaucracy, slow-moving, and resistant to general innovation, I struggled. Where previous leaders had seen my recommendations for innovations and streamlining as huge wins and value-adds, I was told instead to stay within my scope. When making proposals for automations and collaborations, I was advised to keep my head down. When I tried to network and build relationships, I was told that wasn't how things were done.

Suddenly, all of the skills that had made me a star employee for a decade were becoming negative strikes against me in the bigger company culture. While my boss was a great person, and debatably one of the smartest people I had ever worked with, suddenly I was forced to play the game without my skills in my arsenal. I had to set aside my natural inclinations and strengths, and try to build up weaknesses that were more valued. It was beyond painful.

Now, I would be remiss to say that this period in my career was a waste: I learned more about corporate politics and playing the game in this role than in the rest of my work history combined, and it catapulted me forward into my new career of coaching individuals to find their own career success. I am very thankful for that.

But I was in a job mismatch. The value and strengths that I brought to an organization and to my team were basically worthless. I had to change to fit in. This is where each of us is faced with a crossroads.

In a situation where you are a mismatch, you *can* choose to displace and stifle your strengths, build up weaknesses that are more valued, and adjust your communication style to compensate. I have seen people make this choice and find a lot of success. It *is* possible, though it is painful and requires a lot of time investment and intention. It is much harder to strengthen a weakness than it is to turn a strength into greatness.

Your other option is to leave and find a better fit for your strengths somewhere else. Generally, this path is easier to follow and allows for a bit more authenticity in your work and to your person. It would be much harder for me to stifle my results orientation and build up my communication to fit the culture, than for me to leave the company and find a smaller organization in chaos that would benefit from my skills.

While there is nothing wrong with either of these approaches, it is important to evaluate which one will be better for you in the long term. Considerations may include support of your direct supervisor and leadership (if you have a large amount of support despite being a mismatch, it might be worth trying to build up your weaknesses), pay/title (if the role gets you closer to where you want to be long-term, it might be worth sticking out for two or three years), and toxicity (a toxic work environment will ruin your life faster than a bad relationship).

Karen was a high-achieving coworker of mine. She was incredibly capable and spiked in technical and professional expertise as well as innovation. She had already established a pretty successful career before we worked together and was close to obtaining her director title. She had been transferred into our organization to bring her great skillset during a time of massive change in the company.

While I enjoyed working with her and she had a good reputation across the company, our leadership at the time was really looking for quick results and help with change management. Their intention was for her to assist in innovating technology to match the pace of operational change using her technical ability, but the reality was that no one had time to help her develop or execute a tech improvement strategy. While her spikes were needed on paper by upper leadership, our direct manager didn't value them, instead placing emphasis on keeping the technology the same until we could stabilize the business.

This led to boredom and lack of scope for Karen. She wasn't able to innovate or display her technical acumen, ultimately leading to disagreements and poor performance reviews from our boss. Over some candid coffee chats, I encouraged her to look for an internal transfer, but she was determined to prove herself, committing instead to changing her spikes to fit the needs of our management team.

In the short term, things did improve (this is a great strategy if you're trying to buy yourself some time while you look for other jobs), until suddenly things weren't working anymore. Karen was fed up with being told to keep things as they were and feeling undervalued, and our manager was frustrated with the frequent efforts to improve the technology that Karen was proposing. Things very quickly turned toxic, with many meetings ending in yelling matches and tense disagreements. In the end Karen ended up having to leave the firm before she reached her goal of promotion, due to a mismatch of needed skills in her specific team.

This is why it is incredibly important to understand both your strengths and the needs of your organization—to figure out if you are in the right place or on the right track. This is key to developing your long-term career strategy, which will give you fulfillment, success, and your personal brand—which we discuss more in the next chapter.

CHAPTER 4

Brand Building

Branding

/brandiNG/ noun: branding

The promotion of a particular product, person, or company by means of advertising and distinctive design.

You are the entrepreneur CEO of your own career. You have the ability to create, manage, scale, change, and grow your career as your own business in which *you* are the product. While sometimes it might feel as though you are a simple cog in the machine of your organization, the reality is that you are a business owner who only sells one thing: yourself.

One of the most common mistakes that I see is individuals not understanding their skills, value, or impact to their organization and thus not identifying, establishing, and cementing their personal brand. This is the fastest way to devalue yourself within your current team (short term) and the job market (long term). You cannot rely on your tasks and technical work to 'sell' you to your boss, coworkers, or potential employers. Instead, you must build your brand in such a way that it easily sells itself.

When you think of a particular brand, there is likely a tagline or a set of products that come to mind. Let's use Nike as an example: 'Just do it,' Air Jordans, and the old school Gatorade commercials may be running through your head as you read, and that is no accident. Through years of visual communication, targeted messaging, and consistent language, brands create the perception that they want their consumers to have. We, the consumers, find ourselves using the language that they have led us to use when describing their products or their company through subtle, but effective, brainwashing.

When we begin to think of ourselves as a *brand* in the workplace—rather than merely an employee—and identify the cornerstones of that brand, we can create consistent language in the ways we describe ourselves and our work that will lead to greater impact and executive support. In the last chapter, you completed the self-assessment and came to understand your own skills, including the ones in which you spiked in aptitude. In this chapter we will put those spikes together along with a list of 11 items—appropriately titled the '11-List' to create your personal brand.

The 11-List

To create your 11-List, write out the following:

- Five things you want to be known for at work.
- Five things you *don't* want to be known for at work.
- One mission statement.

I first created my 11-List more than ten years ago, and I still keep a copy in my desk today. This list will become the rubric by which you evaluate your performance as well as the strength and fortitude of your personal brand. My list looks like this:

- Five things I want to be known for at work:
    - Strategy/vision
    - Improving/streamlining
    - Being a great leader of teams
    - Passion
    - Strong communication/being articulate

- Five things I *don't* want to be known for at work:
    - Selfishness
    - Micromanaging
    - Shortsightedness
    - Stealing credit for others' work
    - Bad leadership

- One mission statement:
    - I want to help companies solve complex problems and drive improved efficiencies while building the next generation of leaders.

The 11-List is going to be incredibly helpful throughout your career in a few ways. To start, if you compare the things you want to be known for with your spikes from Chapter 3, I bet you see some alignment. People who value productivity tend to score higher on results orientation, while people who value authenticity and empathy in the workplace tend to score higher on integrity and high moral character.

When you put the five things you want to be together with the things you actually are (your spikes) you can craft a personal brand that will align more closely with your skills and values. But a word of advice when performing this exercise: The goal is not to create a personal brand that is vastly different from who you naturally are (even if you may want to). You want to stick closely to what you *are* good at and then become *great*.

If you score middle of the road on 'Drives for results' and 'High integrity/honesty,' but spike in 'Technical/professional experience' and 'Solves problems/analyses issues,' you would not want to create a brand that says you are 'a results-oriented powerhouse focused on delivering for the company with the customer's values in mind.' This would be a misalignment to your actual scores. Instead, you would want a personal brand of 'a subject matter expert with a high level of detailed knowledge that allows you to solve complex problems on behalf of your company and customers.' This brand will be easier for you to live up to.

Take my personal brand for example. In my career, I have been told more than once that I am hard to manage. Not because I am negative or have a difficult personality, but because my productivity level is so high; it can be really difficult for managers to keep me challenged and engaged. As a result, I often become the resource who is thrown into the company's 'black holes' where leadership knows there are issues but has no idea what's behind them or how to fix them.

If you reflect on my 11-List, this aligns closely with things I want to be known for at work, including strategy, streamlining, passion, and being articulate. I would be unable to solve complex issues if I was not passionate or focused on streamlining, and my leadership wouldn't know about my efforts if I wasn't strategic or articulate. The ways I want to be known at work show up in the way leaders describe me.

This also aligns with my spikes of 'Drives for results,' 'Solves problems/analyzes issues,' and 'Champions change.' You can see a consistent thread between these spikes, the ways I want to show up at work, and the feedback I receive from my manager. These three things together create my personal brand and professional reputation.

The exercise of creating your personal brand or mission statement can take some iterating before it is just right. While this is something I often help clients achieve, you can do it on your own as well. The mission statement does not have to be a life purpose wrapped up in a goal and tied with a bow (let's not get overzealous here), it is instead intended to be a representation of essentially how you would like to be known across the workplace.

I've noticed that completing this exercise often leads my clients to make negative comments about their career when comparing it to their mission statement. They want a mission that is community based or gives back in some way, and while that may be true for some, not all of us will build careers in non-profits or with community as the primary focus—and that is okay. Using your skills to further your team and business in alignment with your natural skills and passions while carving a life for yourself that brings you satisfaction is a good thing. And if it makes you feel better, you can think of your mission statement as more like *Mission Impossible*: Your mission, should you choose to accept it, is to further your entrepreneurial business by scaling the career ladder.

Once you understand yourself *as you are*, not as you would like to be, you can begin to better articulate the value that you bring to your team and company in a way that will propel you forward faster.

This ability to articulate your value underpins our next secret.

Secret #10: What people think of you at work is directly in your control

I know that this is a controversial statement. Everyone is entitled to their own opinion, and there will be times that people form an opinion about you that is based on their pre-conceived notions rather than facts. But if you think of a corporation as a hive mind, or at least a hive where very few people's opinions ultimately matter, you can intentionally and directly influence the way those people think about you.

Keep your brand message on the tip of your tongue

When you have, and know, your personal brand, you should describe your work consistently and frequently within the bounds of that brand. The best way to do this is to create and memorize your one-or-two sentence personal brand or mission statement. I gave some examples of what this may look like, but craft one that closely aligns to your skills and values as well as resonates with you and how you feel about your career.

Mine is:

> I am the individual who you put in the black hole of your business, where you have no idea what is going on; I bring organization, results, and clarity to that part of the business so that it can scale. I do this as a passionate people leader who is focused on creating the next generation of great leaders for the company.

If you are in an interview and someone asks about your work experience, that elevator pitch of your personal brand should be the first thing out of your mouth, then you can backtrack over your experience and highlight ways that you have demonstrated that over the course of your career. If you are networking with a new connection and they ask what you do, your elevator pitch should lead, and your title should follow. If you are doing coffee chats in a new company, you guessed it—elevator pitch first, how you can help them second.

This delivery will become more comfortable after a while; by about the 20th time it will be second nature. You will also learn how to say the same thing using different words, so as not to sound repetitive to individuals you talk to frequently. I also recommend picking out three to five words or phrases from your mission statement that you can write on a sticky note and keep somewhere accessible as a workplace reference.

Some examples of this for me might look like:

- "I am excited to have been brought in on this project. My goal here is to help get things organized and deliver fast results with you all. Please let me know how to best support you."

- "Thank you for the opportunity to expand my team. As you know, I care deeply about the next generation of leaders and hope that this individual can scale quickly."
- "This problem seems a bit like a black hole with very little organization. I'd love to help impact that part of the business by bringing some organization."

If you've never done this, or even thought about it, that is okay—for some reason no one teaches us these things (until now). But the individuals with the fastest trajectories know who they are and why they are valuable—and they talk about it often. This sets them apart from their peers, especially when they follow through on delivering on that personal brand for their—and the company's—success.

All of this being said, you do not have to stand up in a meeting and shout from the rooftops, "I am great at customer communication!" I don't want you to be that sleazy car salesman talking about how great he is all the time (if you're in car sales, dear Reader, I'm sure you're the industry's lone remaining humble, high-integrity representative). Instead, you will weave your brand into introduction meetings, kick-offs for new projects, and accomplishment discussions with your boss (more on this in Chapter 5), alongside the impact and value you are adding to the company. This is a winning combination.

Any individual who has managed me in the last ten years would say, "Kendall really knows how to deliver results and communicate effectively. I throw her into the problems no one can figure out." All of them. Probably with that exact same language. Why? Because I describe my works, efforts, and value that way *all the time*, then they see the outputs that align with that brand, and it cements it in their brains.

According to Marvin Minsky, author of *The Emotion Machine*, this echo effect "can be very important when building likability, comfort, and social connections. When people use the same words, it creates less social distance between them and makes them feel more similar to each other."[2]

We experience this every day in the workplace. This is why people can make fun of corporate jargon on social media and everyone relates, because we are all using the same words to describe things. But don't worry, we will 'circle back' to this later (just kidding).

I have a good friend who describes the things she likes or that are going well as 'Gucci.' This is a more popular colloquialism in recent years, but not very common amongst the rest of my friends or coworkers, so I only really hear it when I am spending a lot of time with her. I can count on one hand the number of times I had said the word Gucci before meeting her, but I find myself saying it all the time in the days following my visits to her. I am parroting back her vernacular.

When you describe yourself and your work consistently, using the same or similar language, the people around you start to describe you the same way. They essentially echo your brand back to you, and to others, expanding the reach of your brand and influence.

Have you ever been working on a project and a new person is added to the project team? How does the group respond? Do they say things like "Oh I'm glad they're bringing her in, she's great at [X]," or things like "Ugh, that guy is so difficult"? Either way, this reaction is a product of personal brand, and secret #11.

Secret #11: Your brand will enter the room long before you do and leave long after you are gone

Love it or hate it, 95% of the conversations regarding your career, progression, and growth will happen when you are not in the room. Leaders who are looking for new people to join their team will have conversations with their direct reports, managers wanting to promote within their team will discuss with their boss, and 9-Box conversations (more on this in Chapter 6) will happen with a select group of executives and managers that may not even include your boss.

In the end, your career progression will be determined when you are not around. However, this does not mean that you don't have control over what happens (remember Secret #3?), but it requires a strong personal brand and influence over the hive mind, which I mentioned earlier.

Let your brand do the heavy lifting for you

Your goal is that, when people have new opportunities in their teams or are discussing possible promotions, one person in the room will mention your personal brand positively and everyone else will nod in agreement. Even without you present to describe yourself or to talk about all the good work you've done, you want your personal brand in attendance and corroborated by the other leaders.

I once worked for a company that reserved all talent conversations for vice presidents and above. This meant that even directors managing large teams were unable to represent their people in progression, evaluation, and potential reviews. Most people being discussed in these evaluations were two, three, or even four layers of seniority removed from the individuals in that room.

To assess these team members, executives performed a few different evaluations. First, they scored individuals on familiarity (essentially how well known was each person being discussed). Then they considered scores and performance reviews sent in by each employee's direct manager. Lastly, each candidate for promotion required an 'executive sponsor' who was willing to defend a candidate on their behalf.

It was a fairly thorough and exhaustive process, which I personally much prefer over the single-point-of-failure method that some companies use, but it ultimately meant that leaders and employees were unable to defend their stance in the final conversations that would determine their futures. It required candidates to have a strong personal brand if they wanted to stand any chance of promotion.

The first year I was a manager, I advocated for a promotion in my team. I believed the candidate to be a slam dunk. He had a personal brand of technical acumen as well as strong communication skills and took personal ownership. He interacted regularly with the VPs in that room and had displayed, in my opinion, more than the qualities required for him to move to the next level.

When it came time to submit the formal paperwork, I learned for the first time that he would need an executive sponsor. No one had shared that information with me during the time I had been managing this individual (or even let me know that it would be required for any of my own future upward mobility). Suddenly I was nervous. Despite the fact that I felt this team member was ready, had we done a good enough job with his personal brand that a VP outside of our division would be willing to advocate for him?

Interestingly, that day an executive messaged me asking whether this individual was going up for promotion. I answered yes, but I hadn't realized he would need an executive sponsor. The VP offered to represent. Over the next 24 hours four VPs from different areas of the business reached out and offered to sponsor him. His personal brand had preceded him, and many leaders were eager to advocate on his behalf.

I share this story because even though neither this individual nor I, his manager, had known he would need a sponsor, we had been consistently building his brand and ensuring he had opportunities to prove it accurate. He had demonstrated his value to a broad enough audience, with a high enough level of consistency, making him a shoe-in for the promotion he deserved. While in a perfect world his great work *should* have been enough alone to get him promoted, in reality it wouldn't have been. Instead, his brand was the clincher that differentiated him from his peers and pushed his promotion through.

What is additionally interesting about this case is that the candidate struggled immensely with imposter syndrome. While I believed him to be a great asset and natural born leader within my team, he struggled to perceive himself the same way, often building up his nerves and anxiety ahead of big presentations or meetings.

Pretty much everyone struggles with imposter syndrome at some point in their career. Some apply for a reach job and actually get it, propelling them into a season of second-guessing. Others find themselves sitting in meetings with high-level executives and questioning everything they thought they knew. Or they have a toxic leader for a time, which chips away at their self-worth and leaves behind lasting trauma.

If you're struggling with imposter syndrome, know that it is perfectly natural. I've worked with CEOs and CFOs who also questioned themselves and their abilities, but the key is that they pushed themselves and worked through it by reframing the concepts of confidence and imposter syndrome entirely.

What if I told you that imposter syndrome is not a lack of confidence, but instead a lack of faith in yourself to learn new things? How would that change your perception of your current circumstances?

Confidence is merely the belief in yourself that you can do something—and this includes scaling and learning new things. When you are feeling imposter syndrome, it is not just about feeling as though you don't have the answer in the moment, it stretches deeper to the belief that you cannot learn the skills to perform your job well in the necessary amount of time. But fun fact: you can.

If you switch your mindset away from only being confident when you feel you can do all things perfectly, and instead start to be confident in your ability to learn new things well, you can shift out of an imposter syndrome mindset and step into a stronger executive presence. Your ability to learn the new skills, meet new people, and establish effective communication styles over time will allow you to build success in your role and in your career. Identify the gaps in your current knowledge set (whether those are skills or people) and make a plan to close those gaps (perhaps by using this book as a guide), then come up with some key phrases to help you in the interim in case you don't have the answer right away. Here are some of my favorites:

- Circle back: "That is a great question, thanks for bringing it up. I'm fairly positive the answer is [X], but let me confirm that's accurate with my team and I'll send a follow-up after this call."
- Buy some time: "That's an interesting perspective we'd not explored before. Let me bring the stakeholders together to deliberate and we'll provide an update by [X-day]."
- Delegate to the expert: "That's a good question, and I can see why it's relevant. [Colleague X], you're the expert in that space, are you able to answer?"

Once you have a plan in place to close your knowledge gaps and answers ready for questions you can't yet answer exhaustively, make a list of ten things you are good at in your work that are applicable to your current job or project. Use this as a reference when you forget how amazing you are and start to spiral. Not only can you *do* this work, you *can learn* to do it better, too.

When you have done the diligence in understanding yourself and building your personal brand, it is important to understand the ways that this brand will influence and interact with your progression. Similar to the above example, there will be times when having a strategic and pervasive brand can be the differentiator between career progression or stagnation. In order to optimize this branding strategy, you need to understand competencies and performance reviews.

CHAPTER 5

Competencies and Performance Reviews

com·pe·tence
/kämpəd(ə)ns/ noun
the ability to do something successfully or efficiently.

ALMOST EVERY MAJOR company I have ever interacted with, whether that be through my personal employment or that of my clients, has a way of evaluating the performance of their employees. This evaluation process often takes place behind closed doors (as we mentioned earlier), involving a mysterious set of criteria and a lot of subjective opinions. You need to understand your employer's requirements, often referred to as competencies, as well as the expectations surrounding them, to maximize your chances of progressing in your job.

Some companies will publish these expectations in terms of job architecture, seniority competencies, or job performance expectations. Before you go any further in this chapter, you should email your manager or contact in HR to request a copy of the competencies for your role. While it is entirely possible your company doesn't have them, if they do you want to ensure you get your hands on a copy as soon as possible. If they don't, you want to spend enough time gaining clarity and documenting expectations with your direct leadership to ensure there isn't a mismatch when aiming to reach the required skills of your next level of progression.

If you are in the lucky group whose company publishes their expectations, congratulations! You now have the tools to play the career game on your terms. If your company does not publish their competencies, here is a high-level example for you:

Competency: Job knowledge

Senior associate: Shows a basic understanding of how to perform routine assignments. Occasionally requires assistance from supervisor or others in order to complete task due to lack of knowledge of applicable procedures. Appears to work based on direct assignment from manager. Requires high levels of supervision to effectively complete job duties.

Manager: Has mastered the application of most procedures and processes required for fully successful job performance. In those areas where additional knowledge and expertise are required, satisfactory or better progress is being demonstrated toward their attainment. Requires above average level of supervision on most tasks to be effective. Has demonstrated desire to acquire additional skills/knowledge that will allow them to contribute to the fulfillment of the department's goals.

Senior manager: Demonstrates a basic understanding of all job knowledge skills, procedures and processes;

knows resources to seek guidance for clarification as needed. May seek clarification on new assignments, but once understood does not need additional support and can apply process to a similar assignment. Willing to expand job knowledge with supervisory guidance. Is beginning to think strategically and working to influence their direct team. Has demonstrated desire to acquire additional skills/knowledge that will allow them to contribute to the fulfillment of the department's goals.

Director: Demonstrates thorough understanding of all procedures and processes required to effectively perform all assignments. Very rarely needs help regarding how to execute a given assignment. When new procedures or processes are introduced, learns quickly and begins efficient application. Consistently produces quality work under minimal supervision. Often seeks ways to expand job knowledge to support the mission of the department.

Senior director: Possesses job knowledge that is demonstrated through understanding of how to perform regular work assignments as well as how those assignments relate to other areas. Serves as resource to others regarding work processes and procedures. Significantly exceeds expectations on all tasks. Continuously strives to further improve job knowledge. Constantly solicits feedback from others regarding their performance.

Competency: Leadership and people development

Senior associate: Provides minimal explanation of department mission and strategy when asked. Unwilling to take action without being first told to do so by a peer or supervisor. Waits for others to take action first. Has not become familiar with work environment and available resources.

Manager: Understands most important aspects of department goals. Works well within a team structure and can oversee small teams. Sometimes shows initiative by taking action without being asked or told. When faced with obstacles, often gets 'stuck' in frustration. Generally accepts responsibility for assigned work and performs tasks as directed; however when obstacles prevent a task from being completed, may stop work and wait for direction. Becoming more familiar with work environment and available resources.

Senior manager: Demonstrates an understanding of key goals and mission of department. Develops working relationships in order to complete assignments and ensure consistency within the department. Provides key feedback to team members and encourages their growth in alignment with departmental objectives. Facilitates team-oriented work processes through application of basic project management skills. Works to overcome obstacles but occasionally needs direction and support to succeed. Accepts responsibility for assigned work and performs tasks as directed. Most of the time ensures that results are complete and meet expectations prior to beginning a new assignment.

Director: Demonstrates a thorough understanding of key goals and mission of department. Understands how their professional/technical knowledge, skills, and experience can be applied to fulfill department mission and goals. Is able to find ways to engage others through teamwork. Develops and sustains cooperative working relationships; fosters commitment, team spirit, pride and trust. Always performs assigned tasks as directed. Persistent in overcoming obstacles. Consistently accepts responsibility for assigned work and performs tasks as directed. Always ensures that results are complete and meet expectations prior to beginning a new assignment.

Senior director: Consistently demonstrates knowledge and support of the mission and business plans of the department. Inspires and guides others toward goal accomplishments; consistently develops and sustains cooperative working relationships; fosters commitment, team spirit, pride and trust; shares leadership and helps the team become interdependent by facilitating participation and group interaction. Consistently demonstrates ability and willingness to seize opportunities and resolve problems. Sees what needs to be done and takes appropriate action. Often completes tasks ahead of schedule and provides assistance to others. Understands and demonstrates the ability to effectively prioritize assignments to make the most efficient use of time and resources.

Competency: Problem-solving/decision-making

Senior associate: At times, decisions are hastily made without fully considering the possible consequences. Problem solving efforts may not take into account entire team vision or long-term objectives. Tends to work alone on problems, not soliciting the input of peers or subordinates

Manager: Is transitioning in the area of problem solving and decision making. Has come to understand the need for a more comprehensive approach to reaching solutions and recommending outcomes or taking action. Is willing to listen to a variety of opinions. Demonstrates a willingness to learn from mistakes/failures in order to adapt behavior effectively.

Senior manager: Usually approaches problem solving in a systematic manner. Often seeks resources available for help as necessary. Assures proper documentation and follows up to ensure problem is resolved. Decisions are well thought out and made in a timely manner. Often interacts with a variety of individuals in an assortment of settings. Can accurately assess situational demands and employ appropriate behavioral response.

Director: Always approaches problem solving in a systematic manner. Identifies all resources available for help and involves peers and subordinates as necessary. Tracks issue, keeps management abreast of concerns and follows up to ensure problem does not reoccur. Decisions are well thought out and made in a timely and logical manner. Keeps supervisor informed of progress and results on a regular basis. Effectively follows up to ensure objectives are met.

Senior director: Displays creativity in seeking solutions to problems and in making decisions. Is able to integrate new ideas with current approaches. Effectively identifies potential problems before they arise and acts on problems in the early stages. Once solved, problems do not arise again. Makes good decisions with limited but accurate information while working within schedule.

Actively seeks input when making decisions and openly encourages a diversity of opinions. Possesses a variety of strategies for solving problems.

Competency: Relationship building

Senior associate: Has difficulty building and maintaining good working relationships with others beyond their immediate team. Builds relationships with direct contacts, but does not expand network or influence. Avoids stressful situations.

Manager: Has difficulty building and maintaining good working relationships with others beyond their immediate team. Builds relationships with direct contacts, but does not expand network or influence. Avoids stressful situations.

Senior manager: Develops successful working relationship with others beyond direct scope of team; may need guidance from peers/supervisor in understanding his/her role in being a team player and maintaining a healthy working relationship. Listens well, applying best practices in communication to ensure information is received and understood. Appreciates a variety of inputs but occasionally does not seek other perspectives due to perceived time constraints or project constraints.

Director: Builds and maintains successful working relationships with others. Shows respect for others. Applies active listening skills to most situations. Deals calmly and effectively with stressful situations. Appreciates a variety of perspectives. Builds extensive network outside of direct team to facilitate work and influence the organization.

Senior director: Builds and maintains outstanding working relationships with others. Consistently demonstrates the highest level of understanding, courtesy, tact, empathy, and concern in all interactions. Is sought out by others to provide input into resolving issues between employees. Actively seeks input from relevant sources when making decisions and openly encourages a diversity of opinions. Always willing to listen to multiple perspectives. Excellent at managing stressful situations.

Competency: Communication skills

Senior associate: Generally presents ideas in a clear, concise manner however may not be able to sort 'good to know' from 'must know' information. Not as confident in communications skills. Only occasionally is additional feedback required to ensure understanding of message.

Manager: Effectively communicates with others in speaking and/or writing but may seek advice/editorial input from peers or supervisor. In most cases presents thoughts and ideas in a clear, concise manner.

Senior manager: Communicates with others effectively, in speaking and/or writing. Possesses and uses vocabulary required to successfully express thoughts, ideas and explanations. Presents comprehensive feedback. Keeps supervisor and coworkers informed.

Director: Demonstrates oral and/or written communications skills that result in very clear and concise messages and feedback. Exhibits the ability to explain or describe in a manner that is easily understood by most recipients.

Senior director: Is able to communicate effectively across various levels of seniority and simplify concepts for the correct audience. Has excellent written and oral communication skills and leverages their influence to target communication styles to the audience. Asks strong clarifying questions to drive good outcomes.

Competency: Culture building

Senior associate: Unwilling to take action without being first told to do so by a peer or supervisor. Waits for others to take action first. Requires high levels of supervision to effectively complete job duties. May tend to lose sight of desired end results by becoming too immersed in project or process detail.

Manager: Sometimes attempts to take action without being asked or told. When faced with obstacles, often gets 'stuck' in frustration. Requires above average level of supervision on most tasks to be effective. Is learning to appreciate the significance of goal setting and achievement. Is beginning to show understanding of scope of strategic initiatives and the relationship to shorter term goals.

Senior manager: Often takes action without being asked or told by a peer or supervisor. When faced with obstacles either finds a course of action or seeks guidance to overcome. Generally produces quality work under minimal supervision. Is goal-oriented but may need assistance in prioritizing resources, projects. Keeps supervisor informed of progress as needed, not in a formal or routine manner. Seeks to understand new policies/initiatives in order to support them and encourage others to do the same.

Director: Frequently takes action without being asked or told by a peer or supervisor. Persistent in overcoming obstacles. Consistently produces quality work under minimal supervision. Always has a comprehensive picture of the end results desired. Is goal-oriented and effectively prioritizes the channeling of available resources. Keeps supervisor informed of progress and results on a regular basis. Effectively follows up to ensure objectives are met. Embraces new policies/initiatives and encourages others.

Senior director: Consistently demonstrates ability and willingness to seize opportunities and resolve problems. Sees what needs to be done and takes appropriate action. Significantly exceeds expectations on all tasks with minimal supervision. Pushes the limits of his or her job toward the achievement of goals. Makes sound judgments about when and where to take risks in order to obtain results. Impacts and influences others in promoting his or her point of view. Reacts immediately and effectively to changes in plans and priorities. Shows exceptional ability when forced to manage through a crisis situation. Views new challenges as opportunities for improvement and embraces change enthusiastically.

As you can see, these competencies exist across both soft and technical skills. For many this is the starting point of workplace confusion. We leave education, an environment where you are graded exclusively on technical skills, with soft skills only impacting your free time or social life, expecting our jobs to function similarly. I would be a millionaire if I had $1 for every time someone told me "I don't care if people like me, I just want to do great work."

Many people approach their career this way: Work comes first, personality is second. And yet, these same people are the first to complain if their boss isn't nice enough, their peers steal credit for their work, or if they aren't included in projects that involve many different groups. They are the first to raise their hands and say soft skills shouldn't matter and the first to hold others accountable for their lack of soft skills (the double standard is real here).

I'm not complaining about these individuals; I was one myself, as I admitted in Chapter 1, but I *am* trying to draw attention to an undeniable truth of the workplace, which is, conveniently, our next secret:

Secret #12: People prefer to work with people that they like

I know, such a bummer, right? That is why five out of the six competencies outlined in the previous table are soft-skills-related (and likely if your company makes their own, you see a similar ratio). We are all collectively scored more so on our ability to collaborate, contribute to culture, and work effectively with others than we are on our technical ability to do a job.

This might come as an 'aha!' moment. You're realizing that for all of your overtime, your training, and your work efforts, you probably failed to address these factors in your delivery and personal brand. That is okay—we'll work together to put you on the shortlist for promotion.

Make sure you know what your boss thinks about your competencies

The biggest push back that I get at this stage in my coaching is, "I don't want to be fake and just kiss butt to get promoted." But that's not what I'm advocating for at all. Instead, I want you to think of communication, delivery, and even personality (to an extent) as learned skills. I want you to realize that once you understand the importance of communication in working effectively, *you* control how you interact with others and how you are perceived, rather than letting the circumstances around you influence your career.

Homework assignment #2

Now that you have your competencies, even if you are using my general ones, you have more homework. Go through them and score yourself against each one. The easiest way I have found to do this is to read all of the competencies for job knowledge and then highlight the box that you think describes you the best. Are you operating at the level of a senior associate? A manager? A director? Then repeat this exercise for each category of competency until you have selected one in each category. Give yourself a score of 5 for senior director, 4 for director, 3 for senior manager, 2 for manager, and 1 for senior associate. Average your scores to get your estimated seniority level.

Then comes the hard part. Give a blank competency chart to your boss and ask them to complete the same exercise of highlighting which boxes they believe describe you. Once you get that feedback from your leader, you can compare it to your self-evaluation to determine your next steps. No matter what, one of the following three scenarios will occur:

1. Your boss scores you higher than you scored yourself *or* at a higher seniority than you currently are: You need to be having targeted conversations regarding your progression. Clearly, they believe

your performance to be where it needs to be for you to operate at a more senior level, so what is holding back your progression? Is it a lack of budget or available positions? If so, what is the timeline over which they expect to be able to remediate that issue and promote you to the associated level? Is it timing? Great, get them to commit to the next promotion cycle. In either of these circumstances, don't stay too long in a position you have outgrown for a manager who won't advocate for you. Give yourself no more than 12 months to end up at the seniority level you are already operating at.

2. Your boss scores you lower than you scored yourself *or* at a lower seniority than you currently are: If it is the latter, you're about to get fired or at a minimum performance managed. No manager will have much patience for an individual who they believe is operating at a level more junior than they are being paid. Your goal in either case is to understand more about where your personal perception mismatches with your boss and create a development plan to close those gaps. If they scored you lower in communication, ask for specific examples and real-time feedback moving forward so that you can understand what component of communication is hurting you and fix it.
3. Your boss's scores roughly match yours overall with some minimal differentiation by category: Good! You and your boss are in sync (you must have done the homework from Chapter 3 before this exercise). You want to close any small gaps (similarly to scenario two) and you want to understand what it takes for you to be highlighted completely at the next level of seniority. Your goal is to get as many highlights in the next seniority category as possible, which will help your boss advocate for your promotion. This means that if you are a manager, you want to be highlighted as senior manager or higher in every category if possible. Then refer to scenario one. My favorite way to do this is ask this question: "What would it take for you to feel comfortable advocating for my promotion on the next cycle? I saw that you scored me manager

level in communication and job knowledge, what would you need to see from me in the next six months to feel as though I am operating as a senior manager in these categories?"

This exercise will give you more insight into how your manager perceives your performance than the last ten one-on-ones you have had. It will also draw attention to the specific areas of improvement you should be investing in, in order to see the progression that you want.

Secret #13: A desire for a promotion without a plan will land you exactly where you are now 12 months in the future

Very (and I mean extremely) rarely will someone get promoted without trying. We all expect our boss to just know that we want to get promoted, give us projects that will help us, and then advocate on our behalf. While there are managers who do that, more often than not the people who get promoted are the ones who asked for it, had a plan, and built their own advocacy resources. They didn't just walk into their year end and get surprised with a promotion and a raise.

As a side note, I believe many managers need to do a better job of setting expectations with the individuals in their teams and communicating promotion paths, but that is a topic for Chapter 10.

If you do not make a plan for your own development, in partnership with your manager, you will not get promoted. That is why the aforementioned exercise is so important; it forces you and your manager into alignment and addresses performance gaps in a non-biased way. It also gives you a platform from which to brag about yourself.

Learn to brag

You heard me right: Brag about yourself. Now before you throw this book across the room with images of the overly confident coworker that you hate running through your mind, I've got a solution that keeps you from being obnoxious. This solution requires two tools and one mindset shift.

The tools are the competency chart we just discussed and my accomplishment tracker (you can get access from my website at thatcareercoach.net/resources). Once you know which areas you are focused on in the competency chart, you can align your projects, tasks, and achievements in your tracker to those categories. With this alignment, you can better evaluate and demonstrate your progress regarding improving in these categories. Remember, you've already heard from your boss exactly what they want to see from you in the next 12 months, and you should be working hard to demonstrate those skills and deliver on those projects.

Now for the mindset shift: You are not bragging, you are informing.

Take a quick second and recap your last workday on a blank sheet of paper. Write out any meetings you attended, work you completed at your desk, coaching you provided another employee, water cooler conversations you had with coworkers, and make it thorough. Then highlight the activities where your boss was present and engaged.

What percentage of your day is highlighted? 20%? 50%? 60%? Odds are it isn't 100% (unless you have an unbelievably dedicated micromanager). That means that for the remaining percentage of work you completed, your boss has no idea what you did or the level of effort required. We're going to focus on that percentage of work.

You must inform your boss of the work you complete and the effort it takes when they are not present. This does not have to be a laundry list of 312 items you completed yesterday, or a detailed excel spreadsheet outlining how every minute of your day was spent, but it does need to include efforts taken to improve the overall company, deliver on major initiatives, and innovate new ideas.

As a senior director in a large financial services company, I had one-on-ones twice a week with my boss, sent monthly recaps of my team's wins, and shared out quarterly business reviews that highlighted the efforts of my division. No one told me to do these things, but I knew that if I didn't inform the organization at large with the efforts my team and I were completing, it would go unrecognized and undervalued.

Secret #14: Work that your boss doesn't know about doesn't matter

You might be contemplating your entire existence in this moment, wondering just how much of your efforts have been wasted over the course of your career. This is why you must inform your boss of your efforts and, more importantly, their impact on the organization. If you do not inform them, they will not know, and you will not get credit.

Cover your… assets

The flipside of informing your boss is covering your… assets. When you mess up at work, do you run to tell your boss? Most people don't, instead hoping that they can resolve the issue quietly without their boss ever finding out. But the reality is that even resolved issues generally make their way up the management chain. It is much better for your reputation if you are the one who informs your boss.

You can do this in two different ways. First, when you make a mistake, come up with a plan to resolve it quickly and inform your boss immediately. It would look something like this:

"Hi. I wanted to make sure that you were informed about a small mistake in the report that went out to the leadership team yesterday. We have already resolved yesterday's data and will resend the report presently. Moving forward, we have done [X, Y, Z] in order to prevent this mistake from occurring again. I just wanted to make you aware in case any questions come your way."

This shows quick problem-solving, ownership of the mistake, and the measures you are taking to prevent it happening again in the future. Once this note is sent, if someone goes to your boss and says, "Kendall messed up yesterday's report. What is going on?" they will be prepared with a clear answer and will be able to defend you rather than immediately turn around and accuse you.

The second way to use this is in a preventative manner. Say that you are working on a project, and you see some red flags starting to form that could become issues in the future. Maybe they are interpersonal conflicts, maybe they are differences of opinions regarding the subject matter, or maybe they are a lack of participation by some key members. Regardless, rather than just having an awareness of the situation, inform your leadership early to prevent negative backlash later. It would look something like this:

"Hi, I wanted to bring something to your attention. Recently in working sessions for the project, I have noticed some tension between [X] and [Y]. They both seem to have good intentions regarding delivery but often present opposing viewpoints and have recently become increasingly charged in discussions. As of now, I have it well in hand and am able to continue progressing the project forward, but I wanted it on your radar in case it escalates and I need to bring you in for some additional support."

This arms your boss with more information in case either of the parties in question go straight to them for resolution or if project issues start to arise in the future. It gets them on your side ahead of time and ensures they don't accidentally step in the middle of an ongoing feud.

Why is all of this important? Because understanding the competencies for your job, how you measure up, and then proactively informing leadership of how you are performing relative to those competencies (while protecting your reputation) are key steps you must take to get promoted and progress your career.

Secret #15: Most conversations about your career will take place without you in the room

For many people, this secret would read '*all* conversations about your career will take place without you in the room,' but once you've started to have targeted progression conversations with your boss it won't be 'all' anymore (sadly now it is just 'most'). Many of the company's conversations regarding progression and putting people in new roles will happen amongst more senior leaders, in a closed room, without you.

Set yourself up for cross-calibration success

Similar to the review that I described in the previous chapter, most companies of significant scale will hold cross-calibrations to evaluate their talent. (While smaller companies might have less formalized conversations and use different terminology, they will consider the same factors we cover here.) A cross-calibration is essentially where leaders bring the reviews of their teams into a room to compare against the reviews of the other teams in the organization. Then they calibrate scores across seniority levels and comparable job types. It is important to understand how these reviews work, both to apply the previous advice effectively and to set yourself up for success in these conversations.

The whole process will happen across several phases, some of which you have a great deal of influence over, and others which you do not. Let's talk through each one.

Performance review

Have you ever been scored on a scale of 1 to 5 at work? Generally, companies will use this scale to represent 1: unacceptable/needs improvement; 3: meets expectations; and 5: exceeds expectations.

They will score employees against the competencies for their role and give the employees in turn a chance to rate themselves. Some companies will also gather peer feedback systemically to assist in the scoring of the individual.

This performance review is about 80% within your control. You can ensure alignment between you and your boss by completing the competency evaluation outlined earlier in this chapter; you can work on high-impact projects and communicate them to your boss effectively; and you can establish a strong personal brand. The remaining 20% will honestly come down to how transparent your boss is with you throughout the year and their dedication to your progression.

Promotion submission

If you are expecting a promotion, or even just hoping for one, this step is about 60% within your control. You should be completing a competency evaluation and discussing your desire to get promoted 6–12 months in advance with your leadership.

Getting alignment with your boss regarding the timing for your promotion, the probability of it happening within your preferred time frame, and clear development opportunities that align with those goals is essential to your promotion taking place. As we have reviewed in this chapter, getting a lot of work done (even the right work) is simply not enough to keep you progressing at the speed and frequency which you desire.

It is also important in this step to understand what the company's requirements for promotion look like. As I outlined in Chapter 4, my company required a sponsor, a clear outline of accomplishments, plans at the next level, and a high-performance review. Google, for example, requires a 'promotion packet' which is essentially a write-up of all your great work, mapped to the company's values and your department's objectives, to be reviewed by a senior leadership panel that won't even include your boss. Once you understand how your company evaluates potential promotions, you can prepare accordingly.

Calibration

The last phase of your performance evaluation is the one where you have the least control: calibration. Once your performance review has been submitted and your company's specific promotion documentation is complete, your manager hands this information to their manager or even-more-senior leadership. They will then sit in a closed room where they evaluate everyone as a group. In this phase, three separate evaluations will take place.

First, an assessment of your network. "Who knows Kendall?" someone will ask, and hands will go up physically around the room (or in an Excel tracker somewhere). The people who know you will then be active participants in your calibration. This is the portion where you have the most influence. You can network proactively and expand your relationships ahead of the meeting to ensure you get more hands at this step (more on how to do this in Chapter 8). Now, there isn't a prize or a special bonus for who has the most hands raised, but it does increase your odds of maintaining a high rating or getting a promotion if many people in the room know you *and* think highly of you.

Secondly, there will be a group assessment of performance reviews. Most companies aim to have 70% of their employees score a 3, with 10% getting 1–2 and 20% getting a 4–5. There is a lot of debate about whether or not this is the correct approach (that would take an entire separate book to sort through), but for the sake of simplicity let's assume that your company follows this bell curve.

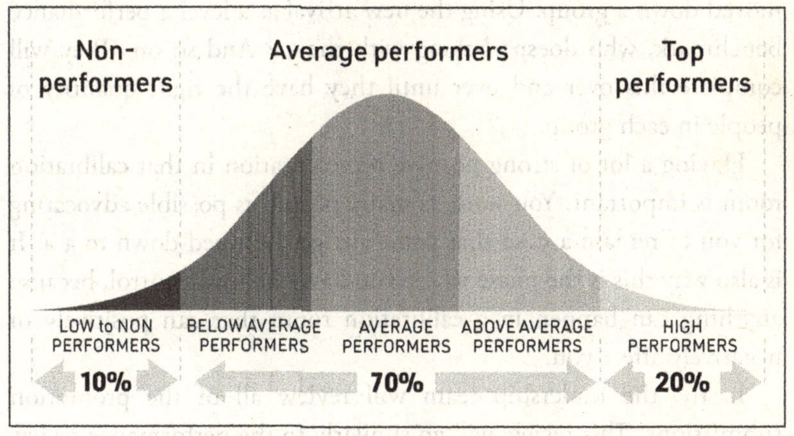

This means that to be a 5, you have to perform better than 90% of your peers at the same seniority level. In this regard, performance reviews are a direct competition. Assume your company has 100 senior managers, of which you are one. Your goal would be to be regarded as one of the top ten best managers in your entire company.

When you put performance reviews in this context, it is easier to understand why you might get a 4 or even a 3. Because how could you stand out so dramatically to end up in the top ten year after year? It isn't probable. And yet many people walk out of their performance reviews frustrated that they didn't get a 5. It's okay, I promise (but more on this in a bit). Most importantly, what happens in this calibration is this exercise: adhering to the bell curve.

Say that all of the submissions given by managers actually put the company at a 5–65–30 split (as opposed to the 10–70–20 ideal). Once leaders get into the calibration room, they will evaluate each group and move people until they fall into compliance with the percentages. The way that they do this is they will look at all the 5s (assume there are 15) and say "Who in this list doesn't perform at the same level as the others? Who are our outliers?" and evaluate each individual until they move five of those people down into the 4 bucket.

Then they will look at the 4s starting with the 5 that they just moved down a group. Using the new arrival as a level 4 performance benchmark, who doesn't belong with the 4s? And so on. They will complete this over and over until they have the right quantity of people in each group.

Having a lot of strong positive representation in that calibration room is important. You want as many people as possible advocating for you to remain a 5, so that you don't get bumped down to a 4. It is also why this is the phase where you have the least control, because anything can happen in a calibration room that can positively or negatively affect you.

Lastly, the leadership team will review all of the promotion submissions. This review will go similarly to the performance review in that they will evaluate all managers up for promotion together to identify any outliers in performance or who may not be ready for the senior manager title when compared to their peers. However, in this calibration your manager's opinions hold far more weight than in the general performance calibration. If your direct boss needs you to get promoted, they have the role and budget for you, and you aren't an outlier, your promotion is likely to be approved.

Now, this is where I see a lot of budget-related blame get thrown around. It is true that companies and teams only set aside a certain amount of money for promotions (that is separate from hiring, which is another topic), and so if in calibrations your position isn't deemed a high-value addition to the company, or if your performance isn't in line with the other promotion candidates, you could be rejected due to budget constraints. But in my professional experience this isn't very common unless your company is actively making layoffs or has a formal promotion freeze. If you've done all of the other steps, then your boss citing budget constraints as the reason you didn't get promoted might be enough of an indicator that it is time for you to start looking for a new job.

CHAPTER 6

The 9-Box

po·ten·tial

adj. /pə'ten(t)SH(ə)l/

having or showing the capacity to become or develop into something in the future.

PEOPLE OFTEN GET confused regarding the difference between their *performance* and their *potential.* The previous chapter covered competencies and performance reviews, primarily focusing on the performance aspect of progression. This is easier to quantify and measure than potential, so companies invest a lot of time and effort into understanding the various performance metrics and comparisons across their organization.

However, potential is a bit more subjective. When leaders evaluate an individual's potential, it is essentially an assessment of how rapidly and how high an individual will progress. This is generally based on a team member's soft skills rather than their technical acumen, and it is harder to build a consistent measure across individuals. Where in a straight meritocracy, performance is the only measure of success, most companies don't operate that way. Instead, they value the soft skills of their employees (perhaps more than technical acumen) and thus attempt to build a more balanced evaluation method.

You might not like hearing this. I often meet clients who want to tell me how unfair it is that they need to work on their soft skills when their technical skills are so strong. But a straight meritocracy has its own issues. Imagine working for someone who is incredibly technically proficient but doesn't know how to communicate what needs to be done or to coach you to grow yourself. This would ultimately lead to micromanagement, the leader always saying, "I'll just do it myself," or a lack of growth and progression for the individuals within that team. In short, they become toxic bosses that are overall bad for the company. While flawed, measuring potential is an attempt to prevent that from happening.

Separate your potential from your performance

Employees expect that their performance is an indicator of their potential, when often the two are unrelated. Being a high performer does not necessarily mean that you will have high potential or even rapid progression (though we would like to think so), which is why it is important to understand the differences between these two measurements and how they will impact your career. The 9-Box is a common talent assessment tool used by many large companies that plots the performance of an individual on one axis and their potential on the other.

These boxes have been titled different things in the various reviews I have sat on, but the essence of each box remains the same across companies and industries.

Performance, which we have already covered in depth, is plotted along the X axis. Potential is plotted along the Y axis. You will often hear managers discuss your performance but rarely your potential; this is treated as a secret review in most organizations and, rather than having clear standards set, it is usually a group-think evaluation.

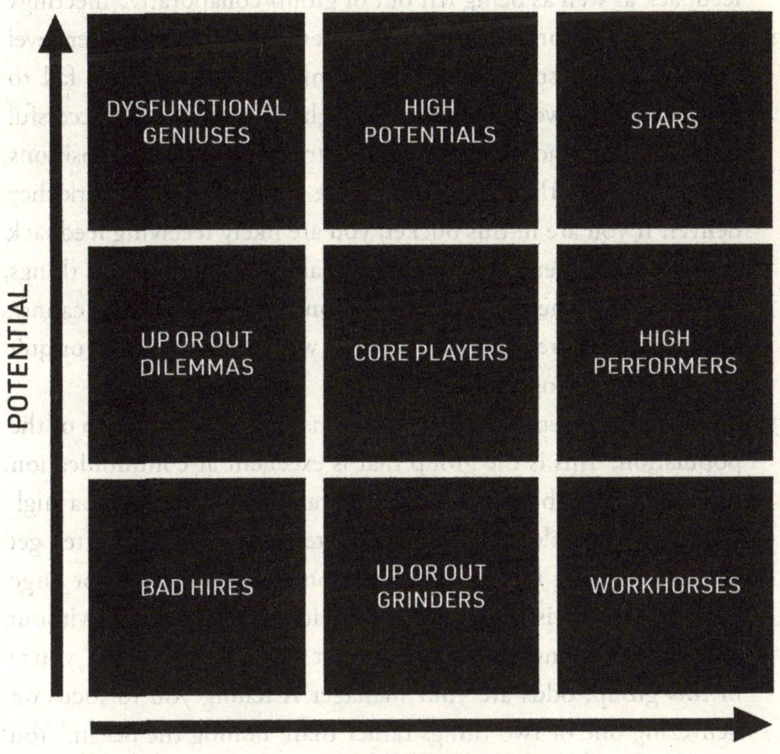

Let's talk through each box in detail so that you can figure out which one applies to you.

The 9-Box:

1. Bad hires: These are the individuals who demonstrate low performance and low potential. They do not execute their core job with a high level of proficiency, nor do they have strong soft skills. No one stays in this box for long. They are either effectively managed into another box or fired. If you are currently sitting in

this box, you are likely receiving a high volume of constructive feedback as well as being left out of group/collaborative meetings.

2. Up or out dilemmas: These team members show a higher level of soft skills, a strong ability to communicate, but they fail to deliver on their work or follow through. They would be successful managers and leaders, yet they get stuck in more junior positions, unable to prove themselves due to the lower quality of work they deliver. If you are in this bucket, you are likely receiving feedback that your manager knows you are capable of doing various things, but that they need to see execution improve. If you cannot improve your core work delivery, you will be managed out or quit due to lack of progression.
3. Dysfunctional geniuses: A snazzy name for a bizarre group of the population. This is the group that is excellent at communication, understands problem-solving and strategy clearly and at a high level, but is unable to deliver their core work. They may often get distracted trying to manage others on the team, push for large strategic enterprises, or come up with multiple ideas without actually delivering anything in their day-to-day job. If you're in this group, odds are your manager is telling you to focus on delivering one or two things rather than 'boiling the ocean.' You will probably leave before you are managed out.
4. Up or out grinders: Sadly I see many people fall into this group. This group is strong in their delivery of their work, occasionally going above and beyond, but with poor communication and self-advocacy skills. This means that they are constantly grinding out their day job but getting little recognition for their efforts. If you are in this group, you likely very rarely receive praise from your leadership and consistently score 3s at the end of the year, but with no indication of a promotion or a raise. This will be very similar to the workhorses group but likely with a more reasonable scope size and less overtime.
5. Workhorses: If you find yourself in this group, your number one priority should be to move up to the high performers box. This

group is similar to the up-or-out grinders but likely with a too-large scope, they are working overtime fairly consistently, and the team cannot operate in their absence. Yet, they are not recognized for these efforts with progression and growth, but instead with even more work. Managers tend to take advantage of people in this box rather than invest in their soft skill development to move them up. If you are in this box, you likely hear "we couldn't do this without you" on a daily basis, and yet you aren't included in meetings with leadership or on cross-collaborative projects.

6. Core players: Managers love core players. When people discuss work-life balance or 'lazy girl jobs' this is likely the space on the 9-Box that they are referring to. These individuals do a good job in their core work, they have good soft skills, they will likely get promoted to middle management with very few issues and then plateau until retirement. They don't work overtime or get overly acknowledged by leadership, but they are the steady-state players that keep the team operating smoothly. If you're in this category, you likely are pulled into many projects, referred to as a subject matter expert (or SME) and score 3–4s on your year-end reviews consistently with little to no overtime.

The next three boxes are the ones that you should be aiming to fall in for your long-term success.

7. High potentials: This group is good at their job and can deliver a strong portfolio of work, but their communication and soft skills outshine their core job performance. They are often brought into high-profile projects and initiatives to collaborate across groups with broad programs, but not assigned a large scope of work or highly detailed projects. They are rarely referred to as a SME but often referred to as a leader or collaborator. If you are in this group, management may struggle with where to place you or may even move you around a lot to focus on whatever the most painful issue

of the day is, but you will consistently get good feedback from your leadership.

8. High performers: An employee in this group is the SME you see in every meeting. Not only do they handle an immense workload, with a high level of proficiency, but they also have strong soft skills and likely move up every 3–4 years. They are every manager's dream because they are able to come in and pick up topics quickly, they rarely (if ever) drop the ball, and they have strong enough soft skills to handle most complex situations and step into management easily. If you are in this group, you likely get 4s and 5s each year and promoted somewhat regularly. Your work is often celebrated slightly more than your leadership skills, but overall you feel appreciated and successful.
9. Stars: This group is *small* (before everyone reading immediately hones in on this group, remember this is 1–5% of the population). This is the group that has excellent soft skills, likely moves up faster than their peers, delivers high-caliber work, and is generally discussed in all talent reviews as the most 'recruited' person across an organization. This person networks naturally and has learned how to play the game successfully. They are also incredibly skilled at navigating interpersonal conflict and high-stress environments. If you are in this group, you know it—and there is no other qualifier.

Generally, companies will not tell you which box you fall into, but you should be able to feel it based on feedback and coaching. This can be somewhat confusing for the average employee, but hopefully the above clarifications have helped you identify your box. If you are struggling to place yourself between two boxes, assume the higher performance or lower potential.

Before you read this and think that 'star' is where you always need to live (and start beating yourself up if you are not currently in that category) I have been a 'star,' a 'high performer,' a 'high potential,' a 'core player,' and a 'dysfunctional genius' over the course of my career. Your box is not fixed permanently, and it will shift over time based on your level of seniority, the investment you make in your own development, your relationship with your manager, and your opportunities to showcase your skills. Most of all, it will depend on your company's culture and its alignment to your personal brand and skills.

Secret #16: Your potential, not your performance, is what gets you into senior leadership

The most common issue that people bring to me in coaching is this: "I am working hard, lots of overtime, and my boss says I am great at my job, but I'm not moving up." If you feel like this resonates with you, you are a 'workhorse,' and that will be the reason you do not move forward. Because it isn't the performance of your core job that contributes to your progression, it is your potential and your soft skills.

Boost the soft skills that will show your potential

Kris was the first person I ever coached. She came to me, struggling deeply with her soft skills and frustrated with her lack of growth. She knew she had a problem but wasn't sure how to articulate it or fix it. She had been suffering for years in a dead-end role with a manager who didn't know how to coach her in her soft skills.

It is much harder for managers to teach soft skills than it is to teach technical. I often see managers recruit with the opposite in mind—looking for a unicorn candidate who has all the technical skills without pausing to understand if their soft skills are at the required level. Please don't make this mistake when hiring. I have made an entire career out of teaching soft skills, and it is far more complicated than teaching technical. You will do your team a disservice if you hire someone expecting to teach them soft skills when you don't know how.

Kris's technical performance was outstanding. She consistently scored higher than her peers on goal and metric attainment, and yet she came in as average on year-end evaluations and performance reviews. When Kris came to me, it took me about 15 minutes to realize that the problem lay in her communication style, not in her ability to execute. So we developed a strategy. We would start by improving her written communication and then progress to verbal afterwards. We would shore up her people management skills as well, to prove her capabilities to her manager.

This is where I developed my email template for dealing with leadership or difficult stakeholders: 'ARSE.' (Yeah. I know. It might have been on purpose.) By following this general structure in her emails, Kris was able to instantly start getting better results.

A—Acknowledge: Thank the recipient for reaching out, formally greet them if they are external or of higher seniority, or just address them in general so that they can feel your authenticity in the communication.

R—Restate the question/ask: Find your own words with which to repeat their question back to them, layer on additional context, or ensure you understand what they need.

S—Solve: Present a solution. Provide a summary of the data, answer a direct question, or directionally provide next steps.

E—Extol: Show appreciation for them reaching out, acknowledge them as an SME (especially if they are a specialist), or remind them that they can reach out with any questions.

Here is this template in practice.

Incoming Email:

Hi Kendall, can you let me know the results of the marketing campaign?

Outgoing Response (ARSE):

Hi Steve,
(A) Thanks so much for reaching out—Dave let me know you would be following up to get a recap.
(R) Last month's marketing campaign regarding the new product launch was a success.
(S) Overall, we have found a 51% open rate and a 2% click rate from this email strategy; I have attached further details for your viewing/utilization.
(E) Please don't hesitate to reach out if you need anything else, I know you are very close to the email campaigns, and I'm happy to provide additional information as needed.

Thank you,
Kendall

In this example, (R) adds context and clarity—it was last month's campaign for the new product—rather than restating the exact question.

Then we focused on improving Kris' verbal communication by introducing two methodologies for better engagement.

First, we started to acknowledge before we respond (we will go deeper into this verbal communication skill in Chapter 9) wherein we ensure others feel heard by acknowledging their opinion and perspective before responding with our own.

Here is what this looks like in practice.

Peer/coworker: "I don't think that this is the best idea. I don't think it will work for the operations team."

Kris (acknowledge): "I appreciate you bringing up the operations group. It's also a high priority for us that this solution would work within their existing processes." (Respond:) "I do feel that we have considered them, as you pointed out, in our testing with their group. It appears as though this recommendation works in all of the scenarios we ran."

This ensures people feel validated rather than steamrolled in favor of your perspective.

Second, we layered on optionality (we'll touch on this again in Chapter 11). Optionality is an exercise in which we propose a set of three solutions rather than sharing only our preferred outcome. This allows stakeholders to weigh in and choose a decision while allowing us to maintain a bit more emotional distance from the ultimate outcome.

In this method, we propose three solutions to any problem.

1. Continuing to do things how we have been doing them: This generally will come with an efficiency, license, or risk cost associated with it.
2. Our preferred solution: This may have a cost associated with it, but long-term it should have a return on investment (ROI) of efficiency, cost, or risk mitigation.
3. Either a hybrid option between solutions one and two *or* an alternate solution that could work: this is a great opportunity to highlight others' perspectives or acknowledge another solution that may work.

Once Kris started working on her soft skills and getting positive feedback from her clients and stakeholders, her boss put her on a highly visible project working across the department. We further honed her skills during that initiative and ultimately were able to help her display her leadership skills in that capacity. Three months later, her long-awaited promotion finally came. When it did, her boss shared this feedback:

> I was glad to see your improvements regarding communication and leadership this year. Your performance has always been strong, but we were hesitant to put you in a leadership position without your communication being equally strong. Now that you have displayed your ability to lead a team and deliver results in that capacity, I feel you have unlimited potential within the team.

This is a clear example of how her performance had always been strong, but her potential was capped by her soft skills. Improving the latter allowed her to finally break through that ceiling and see the results she had wanted all along. Without understanding the types of conversations that were happening behind the scenes, Kris was struggling to understand her lack of progression, but once she understood what was needed and expected, her growth was rapid.

So much of intentional career management, or 'playing the game,' is learning where you stand relative to your company's expectations and your peers. The 9-Box, competency charts, and year-end reviews are some of the ways that you can better understand where you fit into the broader organization. Once you are armed with this information, you can decide how to best advocate for yourself and invest your time into developing your skills for continued upward mobility.

CHAPTER 7

Skill Maturity with Seniority

skill
noun /skil/
the ability to do something well.

WHEN YOU FOLLOW the advice in this book and progress in your career, you will be expected to enhance and strengthen various skills in alignment with your newfound seniority. This expectation of skill development rarely comes with coaching or instruction but is instead a 'learn by doing (and seeing)' phase of your career. The problem with this approach is that many of us struggle to develop skills without clear instruction and guidance, ultimately leading to a plateau in our growth.

In Chapter 3 you learned which of your skills are strongest and uniquely differentiate you and your performance. Generally, these spikes will not change much over the course of your career, but you can, with intention and investment, progress your skills as you move up in seniority to prevent any stagnation. Once you've developed the right skills at the right level, they will start to benefit not only you but your whole workplace ecosystem.

Secret #17: Building your leadership skills allows for not only your success but the success of your team

If you want to be promoted into leadership and potentially continue your progression to the executive level, it is not enough to be good at your job and empower your team to be good at their jobs. You must be continuously growing and developing yourself and your people while ensuring your leadership is informed and educated on the importance of that work. This will allow you to move further in your career and bring your team alongside you with their growth and progression as well. But before you work on your leadership skills, there are several other skill levels you need to master.

Develop the skills needed not only for the level you're working at, but for the levels you aspire to

There are a few common sticking points where progression falters: the rise from individual contributor to manager, manager to leader, and leader to executive. Each of these jumps requires the maturing of a new skillset, which I think of as 'building your toolbox' to prepare you for future opportunities. This skill development takes part in four stages:

1. technical acumen,
2. social skills,
3. managerial capabilities,
4. strategic vision.

This chapter tees up the major methods you will use to keep progressing your career forward, as well as the best investments to make of your time and finances at each stage in your career. The three chapters that follow dive deeper into the major skill jumps that you will have to master, as well as some of my most applicable tactical tips and tools to become proficient in them.

When we look first at technical acumen, this is the skill most important to your progression at the individual contributor and junior levels of work. You must be able to prove sufficient technical abilities in the first few years of your career if you want to move up. There are three main methods here to focus on and two primary financial/time investments.

Methods for enhancing technical acumen

1. Proactivity: This is one of the biggest differentiators at the start of your career for individuals who progress quickly. Rather than waiting for your boss to give you clear step-by-step instructions, start trying things on your own and aim to solve their problems without their hands-on guidance. Then check in with them regularly to ensure you are on the right track, iterating on your deliverables frequently. This will become easier as you learn more context and details about your company and role, but don't be afraid to have ideas, offer up your skills to your boss, and drive the organization forward of your own accord.
2. Core work delivery: This is the day-to-day delivery of your core job. Depending on your role, this could mean creating spreadsheets, managing a system, writing code, delivering campaigns, managing projects, etc. and is your number one focus at this stage. If you are struggling with core work delivery, I recommend getting a mentor one level more senior than you are to help with technical skills specifically. Also ask more qualifying questions from your leadership. Most individuals don't want to ask questions for fear of looking like they don't understand, but this almost ensures you

will deliver a subpar product and hurt yourself in the long run. Some questions you can ask include:

- "What is the expected delivery date for this?"
- "Would you like to do a pre-read ahead of that final date to ensure I am on track?"
- "Who should I go to with questions regarding this task?"
- "Can I understand how this will be used and with what audience?"

3. Email/meeting etiquette: While you don't need expansive soft skills or executive presence at this stage, you do need to understand general email and meeting etiquette. Don't send five emails when their content could have been summarized in one, don't send emails with less than three sentences, and don't schedule meetings that conflict with your attendees' existing obligations. This will save you a lot of unnecessary drama at this stage.

Financial/time investments

4. Certifications: This is the time to be learning. Get certified in your particular skill or system, go to company sponsored training, and force yourself to learn as much as possible about your ideal career. Later on, you will spend your time learning soft skills, but now is the time to learn about your core job.
5. Change jobs (laterally) into multiple divisions/industries: A lot of people will tell you to niche down, move up vertically, and stick to a space. This is *bad* advice. You are better off doing your core job in multiple divisions and industries early on for a few reasons. First, it will make you more marketable later when you can work in multiple divisions and industries with similar high performance. Secondly, it will make your future job search easier because you will be able to do your role for basically any company. Lastly, you will learn more about yourself, your skills, your likes, and your dislikes when you are junior rather than getting to the more senior levels and then having to make a big jump.

Once you have proven your technical acumen for your job type, focus on building social/soft skills. Having good relationships with coworkers and teammates will be a big deciding factor in shifting from individual contributor to manager. Here there are two main methods to focus on and one financial/time investment.

Methods to enhance your social skills

1. Interpersonal relationship building: Get along with your peers. Learn to navigate conflict effectively (disagree without saying no—more on this in Chapter 9) and build strong partnerships that allow you to collaborate well and deliver more work. Build friendships and partnerships with your peers that you can rely on to help you continue your progression. This doesn't mean that *all* of your coworkers need to become your best friends, that you should be gossiping or oversharing details about your personal life. Just that you should be focused on building working relationships with the individuals around you to allow you to be more successful in your career, even if on a personal level you aren't friends.
2. Networking: Meet your leadership, the influential people in your organization, and leaders you may one day want to work for with intention. People change companies all the time, but your next career could depend on a relationship you build now. After my first corporate job, I have only once taken a new role where it was not a referral from someone in my network. Don't be fake or inauthentic, but instead focus on learning as much as you can from the senior leadership you have access to (more on this in Chapter 8).

Financial/time investment

1. Mentoring: Get a mentor and learn to mentor others. This is a time investment, but it is worth it at this stage. Studies show we become better at skills when we teach them to someone else, so

mentoring someone else can help you progress your own career too. Additionally, it tees you up as having unofficial management experience when the time comes for you to apply for management jobs. Not to mention, I learned more from mentors than I did from any boss I ever had. Take advantage of the free support.

The next stage is managerial capabilities. Roughly 30% of the population will get stuck at this jump and plateau as a high-performing individual contributor. To overcome this obstacle there are four methods and three financial/time investments.

Methods to jump into management

1. Management: How do you guide and manage your team? Build a good team structure that allows others to develop and grow, have clear streams of work, and talk to your team regularly. Before becoming a manager, you can apply this by leading cross-functional projects, taking on mentees, and having general leadership communication/skills that are displayed through the delivery of your core job. What you shouldn't do is start 'managing' your peers in order to display leadership skills unless explicitly asked by your manager to do so.
2. Setting expectations: Set clear expectations, milestone check-ins, and provide ample context so that your team can meet your expectations effectively. Offering too much autonomy is bad at the initial levels of management if your team is very junior and doesn't have the context yet to run with things well. It becomes your responsibility to set good expectations for two reasons:
   a. Team members can operate with more autonomy and manage their time more effectively.
   b. You will avoid falling into the trap of micromanagement because all expectations and check-ins are set ahead of time.
3. Delegation: Get used to not doing everything yourself. Rather than thinking about this as offloading tasks, instead think of it as

giving other people in your team the chance to shine with their work. If you do everything, they can do nothing, and you will hurt their progression. If this is a skill you particularly struggle with, start first with delegating non-time-sensitive tasks to your top-performing team members. This gives them (and you) the highest chance of success and will reinforce your delegation skills in a safe environment. Then you can expand delegation to your entire team, shifting the time-sensitive tasks to your top performers and non-time-sensitive tasks to the remainder of your team until you build comprehensive skill.

4. Leadership: Figure out where you are leading your team, and how it fits in with their individual goals and objectives. This requires relationships with and understanding of the individuals within your team. Not every person wants to be managed the same way or will be successful in the same tasks. Instead, by learning about the individuals within your team, you are able to play to each of their strengths and make the team operate more effectively overall.

Financial/time investment

1. Coaching/management training: On average, managers receive formal training 11 years after they start managing people; don't let this be you. Instead seek out a leadership coach, management program, or training that will help you start off strong. This stage is ripe with mistakes; avoid as many as you can by being prepared.
2. Books/podcasts: Digest as much information as possible at this stage. Once you hit middle management and beyond, much of your personal and skill development will depend on your intention and time investment. There are many great books on management. Some of my favorites include:
    - *The Unspoken Truths for Career Success* by Tessa White
    - *The New Extraordinary Leader* by John Zenger and Joseph Folkman
    - *The Coaching Habit* by Michael Stanier

3. I'd also recommend that you listen to great podcasts like:
   - *Secrets of the Career Game* (of course!)
   - *The Awakened CEO*
   - *Dare to Lead*

Through the development and application of each of these methods, you will likely progress to middle or upper-middle management. That is great! And many people are happy staying at that level. But if you have aspirations to keep growing and get to the executive level, you will need more of a mindset shift.

One of the most difficult jumps to make (arguably the *most* difficult) is to the director level. This requires not only that you have mastered the first three skill levels, but also that you start to develop strategic vision. This skill is harder to define and harder still to prove that you possess, but we can start by applying three methods and making one financial/time investment.

Methods to jump to executive leadership

1. Developing a strategy: Ask yourself this question: "How would I run my team if I had unlimited money and resources?" Once you know the answer to that, you can walk back to how the team is operating today and create a roadmap to that future state. You can identify the low-hanging fruit that could be resolved easily, as well as the high-ticket items that would be game changers for your team and your organization. Then build your team around this vision to achieve those goals with the resources that you have and develop a concrete plan to fill in any skill gaps that you have for that target-state vision. Communicate this strategy and direction with your leadership so that there is alignment and appreciation for the efforts and direction of your organization.
2. Creating a strong personal/team brand: Knowing who you are, what makes you unique and successful, and how to communicate it effectively is crucial at this level. You must build a strong

reputation for yourself and your ability to lead to have influence and success at the director level. Then you must expand this brand building to your broader team so that the organization has an appreciation for your team and their hard work. The best way, in my experience, to create this team brand is to have a collaborative team strategy session in which you outline the above strategy, pull together the individual brands within your team, and work together to create a one-or-two-sentence summary of the team that everyone can agree on.

3. An appetite for the unknown: You will make decisions, decide direction, and lead organizations that are doing things you've never done at this level. You will have to get comfortable choosing the best possible direction with limited information on a regular basis and consistently step into the unknown. Once you can do this, take ownership for your mistakes (and those of your team), and walk confidently into that space, you will find success.

Financial/time investment

1. Coach: At this stage in your career, I would say it is almost a requirement to have a coach. Those who have outside counsel and guidance at this level have the highest likelihood of success and the best chance at achieving their goals.

While not every team you manage will be in a state of evolution and change, at the director level it is sometimes required to lead an organization through shifts. One of the best moments of my career was during one such shift, where I was simultaneously building and evolving a team to support a growing organization.

During this role, I was taking a very tenured, well-structured team from a manual processing stage, to one of automation, business intelligence, and overall growth. This required implementing all of the leadership skills we've just covered: developing a multi-year strategy in which the team could process five times as much volume without having to grow in size and with less manual involvement, creating a team brand centered around automation and excellence in delivery, and making (what felt like daily) decisions with limited direction or support in order to keep the team progressing forward.

For me personally, this was one of the most rewarding stages in my career because I was allowed to operate with a high level of autonomy and really build a solution from scratch while scaling a team (a great alignment to my passion statements), but it was also *scary* on a regular basis. I was operating without a safety net and there was no one to take ownership of mistakes except for me. It required the rapid mastery of these skills in order to be successful.

By the end of the third year, the team had grown by only a single headcount to support this vision, and had simultaneously scaled in skills, seniority, and acumen to deliver more than double the volume that had been managed at the onset while also establishing the processes to scale even further. The team's brand had shifted from one based on tedious manual processing to one pioneering automation and scale. Not only was I freed up to run my business more effectively, but we were able to deliver additional scale to my boss and his leadership. That results orientation ensured that the team was well compensated, promoted, and given high visibility work to further their own careers.

I was able to achieve these results only because I had put in the time and effort to master the methods and skills we've covered here. Once you too feel confident in these, you need to identify opportunities to display them to your organization. I've given some examples already, but projects that help you get promoted and show off your skills often include:

- Cross-functional, large-scale projects,
- Formal mentorship programs,
- Diversity, equity, and inclusion/culture initiatives,
- Your own ideas that help your team/company operate better,
- High visibility/profile projects.

If you are looking at this list and thinking, 'That's great, but how do I get on these projects?' in some cases you can work directly with your manager and *their* manager to be assigned to these types of initiatives, but, more often than not, it requires the establishment, maintenance, and expansiveness of a strong professional network.

CHAPTER 8

The Network

Networking

/ net·work·ing/ noun

the exchange of information or services among individuals, groups, or institutions

MANY OF THE promotion conversations that take place behind closed doors are little more than popularity contests backed up with performance and potential evaluation data (which we covered in Chapters 5 and 6). The conclusion is that your progression will often rely on leaders from within your area knowing who you are, what you're good at, and what you are capable of. It is not enough to depend on your manager to advocate on your behalf. In short, you're going to need to build yourself a network.

Think of your network like a tree: The trunk of the tree is your direct leadership (your boss, their boss, and so on, vertically up the chain) while the branches and leaves are your relationships laterally, diagonally, and across various organizations. While the trunk is required for a stable foundation and for directional growth, the branches and leaves are what make the tree stand out from its peers and allow it to get the resources it needs (sunlight) to continue to grow. Most people invest a lot of time on a strong trunk, but the discomfort with reaching out across the broader organization hinders them from building the branches.

This lack of a robust network across your company will not only hinder your ability to move directly up the latter, but also severely limit your diagonal and lateral moves across your career lattice. The worst thing that you can do is wait until you need a job (not want one) and then start building relationships with only that selfish motivation in mind. Limiting your network to only your direct peers and stakeholders prevents you from developing foundational relationships that will help you grow.

This mistake is a result of yet another secret you've not been told until now.

Secret #18: Your network must extend beyond your own team

Let me introduce Jim. Jim is the best networker I have ever had the pleasure of knowing. The most impressive statistic that I can share about Jim is this: Jim has never applied for a job.

Jim recently found himself in a dead-end job where he was no longer aligned to his passion statements. His company had undergone a restructuring, and while he had been retained, the new role he found himself affiliated with was not a great fit for his skills or, frankly, his interests. Not knowing where to go next, Jim took a step back to analyze the types of jobs he had held in the past, his recent interests, and where he saw the job market and opportunities going in the future. He carved out for himself an ideal job interacting with tech startups and giving back to his community. The only problem was that his previous experience and education didn't align at all with his newly discovered dream job.

Luckily, it was time for Jim to do what he did best: network. He hosted and attended multiple events in his home city for startups in the surrounding areas, joined newsletters and community groups discussing technology and the startup space, and he did cold outreach to anyone (and I mean anyone) who may have known someone in his newly preferred industry. In the time I worked with Jim he went on five or six coffee chats with complete strangers every week. He would ask them questions about their companies, their roles, and how they liked their jobs. He would offer to connect them with startup founders he had met through events and then solicit feedback from those founders to understand how potential clients viewed his potential employers.

He expanded his network tenfold in only two months and suddenly had connections at five of the biggest players in the industry. When it came time for him to formally look for roles, each of his contacts had potential opportunities for him at varying levels and with differing start dates. Jim had his pick of the litter when it came to jobs and was able to assess the best potential role for himself rather than simply take the first one thrown his way.

Grow your network organically

There are two big takeaways when I look at an individual like Jim. First is that while he was building relationships to ultimately land him the right job, he wasn't approaching people and asking for interviews. He took the time to understand them, their roles, their companies, and to educate them on how he could be valuable to them in exchange. Only after laying this foundation did he approach the job topic. Second is that while many feel networking is an awkward exchange and ultimately uncomfortable, it is key to your long-term success and career progression.

Forbes recently published an article that showcased how more than 45% of roles are filled with someone the hiring manager knows rather than a cold applicant.[3] While this may sound like nepotism to many, the reality is that hiring managers have a higher chance of success when bringing in someone who they know, value, and trust, rather than taking a risk on someone based solely on their resume and interview skills.

While staffing out my own tech strategy team, I filled my open roles almost exclusively with people I knew from previous jobs or who were referred to me by trusted colleagues. I only filled one of the direct reporting roles on my team (out of six) with a cold applicant. While he ultimately was very successful and a great addition to the team, his chances of being selected were far lower than had he reached out and networked with me directly.

This fact highlights another secret about networks.

Secret #19: Without a network you will fail

Having a network does not just relate to getting a job, it is also an intrinsic part of maintaining a job and finding progression. Similar to how Jim networked his way into a new role at a new company, networking allows you to find internal opportunities for development and growth as well as build out an army of advocates who will speak on your behalf during the aforementioned annual reviews. Both of these are invaluable when it comes to playing the game and finding your success.

Grow your network intentionally

So how do you actually build a network? First you need to understand the most powerful people in your organization and create an influencer list of around 20–25 of them who would be important to your network (think your boss' peers, their boss and their peers, senior leaders, etc.) Then score them in accordance with the following template.

Name	Title	Relationship	Seniority	Risk	Power	Exposure	Fear	Validation	Future	Total	Rank

- Relationship:
  - Strong relationship: 5
  - Lukewarm relationship: 3
  - No relationship: 1
- Seniority:
  - More senior than you: 5
  - Same level: 3
  - More junior: 1
- Risk (does this person pose a direct risk to your progression?):
  - No: 5
  - Yes: 1
- Power (how much power does this person exert over the organization? When they speak do people stop to listen?):
  - A lot of direct power: 5
  - Some power with certain audiences: 3
  - No material power: 1
- Exposure (can this person get you a lot of exposure?):
  - Yes: 5
  - No: 1
- Fear (are people afraid of this person?):
  - No: 5
  - Depends: 3 (mercurial personality)
  - Yes: 1

- Validation (does this individual validate certain people or hold the power to be a strong advocate for your initiatives/work?):
  - High validation: 5
  - Low validation: 1
- Future (does this individual have direct power over your progression (leadership chain) or lead a team you may one day be interested in working in?):
  - Lots of influence: 5
  - Could be in certain circumstances: 3
  - No impact to your future: 1

Once you have everyone added and scored, create a total for each person and then rank them. Identify anyone in your list who is more than two levels more senior than you (the equivalent of your boss' boss' boss) and move them into a separate list. In most companies this level of seniority will be considered inaccessible to the average employee, so they are unlikely to form a part of your immediate network. However, it's important to be aware of these people and the influence they hold over your career, so if you *do* have the opportunity to connect with any of these 'reach influencers' whether it be at a happy hour, coffee chat, meeting, etc., *take it*. Don't let an opportunity to build these relationships pass you by.

Return your focus to the top five accessible people remaining in your original list. If you have pre-existing relationships with these individuals, great! You can reach out directly and schedule a mentoring or coffee chat in the next 30 days, or as soon as their calendar can accommodate it.

Depending on the hierarchical nature of your organization, it may be considered uncouth to reach out directly to some of the more senior staff. If that is the case, go to your direct supervisor and say something like the following:

"As part of my desire to continue to grow and develop my skills, I'm trying to expand my network while enhancing my abilities. I've noticed that [X person] is really great at [Y skill]. I would like the opportunity to meet with them to learn more about how I can sharpen that skill as well. Would you be willing to help me make a connection?"

Oftentimes leaders are incredibly supportive of this desire and can help you reach people you may not otherwise have been able to. Additionally, focusing on the skills that the individual possesses that they can transfer to you makes the connection valuable to your boss as well as the mentor. This will ultimately lead to more success than, "Can you help me meet [X person] so that they will advocate for my promotion?"

While this can be easier in an in-person workplace environment, it is still possible virtually; it just requires more intentionality and strategy. When you are in-person, you can make connections more casually in the hallways or swinging by an individual's desk or office (and I highly recommend you do), but when you are working virtually you must send a calendar invite and connect over video chat (with cameras on).

A common problem with intentional networking is that the target individual is so busy that they can't possibly carve out time to talk to you. The reality is that these individuals don't want to waste time, but they likely will make time to coach and mentor, you just need to make it worth their efforts.

This a great point at which to correct a common misconception.

Secret #20: People who help *you* will think of you more fondly than people *you* help

We generally believe that unless we can do something for someone else, our relationship is of no value to that person. While many people can treat their relationships from within this lens (especially in corporate roles), I have found that a little bit of flattering and education can go a long way.

Studies confirm that people tend to trust people they have helped more than they trust people who have helped them. Psychologically, when we provide another person assistance or share our knowledge with them, we tend to view them as an extension of ourselves. We feel as though we have imparted our wisdom to a willing recipient and changed their skillset to mirror our own. Essentially, when we recommend someone we have taught, it is as though we are recommending ourselves.

Allow the people in your network to help *you* first

When you are networking, you should be seeking to learn rather than to help. As a result, the way you structure your conversations should be slightly different than the age old, "How can I help you?"

Each person across your company, especially those with influence and power, will have their own unique brand and skillset. Leaders will comment on how one individual in particular is great at storytelling, or that another is an SME in their area. The best thing that you can do for your current and future development is hone in on the skills of those individuals by identifying their personal brand, and then leverage that knowledge as the platform for building your original relationship while scaling your abilities.

Your first conversation with a new connection, or formalizing a pre-existing relationship, should achieve three things.

1. Learn about the personal and professional background of the other person. What have they experienced over the course of their career and what commonalities do the two of you have?
2. Identify a skill that the individual has that you would like to learn about. "I've noticed that you are exceptionally good at [X skill] and I would love to learn any tips or tricks that you have in that space and maybe come to you for guidance as I develop that skill myself." (This is where a little bit of flattery comes in.)
3. You want to communicate your personal brand and unique skills. This is *not* an interview or a recap of your resume. Instead, this is an opportunity to communicate what makes you a strong team member and differentiate you from your peers.

Once you have established your relationship groundwork, it is important to evaluate your compatibility with that individual. We are all human and have our own personality and communication preferences that will allow us to more easily connect with certain people. If you have a meet and greet with a new person and find yourself uncomfortable or generally not enjoying the conversation, you do not have to meet with this person all the time. If they are in your top five influencers on your intentional networking list, I do still recommend meeting with them formally twice per year. But if you can't bring yourself to do that, eliminate them from the list.

If you connect with that person and find yourself having a very natural conversation, you want to meet with them quarterly at a minimum. These quarterly conversations are your responsibility to prepare for and bring topics for discussion. Likely your influencer is very busy and won't have time to prepare a syllabus of topics to teach and coach you on. You will get far more from your time, and make a better impression, if you come prepared to these conversations with topics they can assist with.

Here are some general rules and discussion prompts you can bring to these meetings.

Rules

- This is not a gripe-fest. This individual still works with you and knows your peers. It is *not* an opportunity to complain about your boss, leadership, or other colleagues. Your goal should be to never share anything negative at all. They are your mentor, not your therapist.
- Come prepared with two or three topics where the mentor can legitimately add value through coaching.
- Always schedule formal meetings and have them on the calendar. This doesn't mean that you cannot stop in the hall and chat with them, but your mentorship needs to be formalized for them to see

it as a professional activity.

- Do not beg for a job. Desperation is a stinky cologne, and you do not want to be emailing them every month asking if they have an available position.
- Counter to the above rule, if they post a new position in their team that you feel you could be a good fit for, absolutely ask them about the position and to be considered *but* do it in a separate call, not during your mentorship session.

Prompts

- Their skill: communication/influence
  - "I'm working with a partner group, and I feel that we have different goals and objectives. How would you approach this situation?"
  - "I find myself struggling with my written communication. What advice do you have for me when sending out recaps or emails?"
  - "I'm trying to drive a project forward, but I am having a hard time getting everyone aligned. What should I be doing differently?"
  - "Can you give me an example where your communication and influence skills really came in handy and how you navigated the situation?"
- Their skill: stakeholder management/conflict resolution/collaboration
  - "There are some different personalities in my team, and I want to learn to communicate effectively with each one. What advice do you have that will help me collaborate effectively?"
  - "I know that you worked with [X team] in the past. What did you do to ensure you had a strong collaboration so that I can emulate it?"
  - "I feel as though I may be experiencing some tension with an individual in my team. How do you recommend I go about resolving it?" (Do not give specifics or name call—if they ask

simply say, "I don't think that the specifics are important. I just want to learn from you on how you address these types of situations so that I can be successful.")

- Their skill: executive presence/presentations/storytelling
  - "I find myself struggling to portray confidence in meetings with leadership. What advice do you have for me?"
  - "Can you take a look at this presentation I am planning to share and give me any advice on the story itself? I know you are a great storyteller."
  - "I want to understand the goals and objectives of this team so that I can be prepared for an upcoming meeting. What can you tell me about them?"
  - "You always appear so confident and prepared. What tips or tricks do you have that I can incorporate into my meetings?"
- Their skill: leadership/management
  - "I'm struggling with delegation in my team. What advice do you have on the subject for a new manager?"
  - "I want to really motivate my team this year to go above and beyond. What are the goals at the top of the organization that I may be able to incorporate?"
  - "I want to really motivate my team this year to go above and beyond. How do you get your team excited for what is to come?"
  - "I have to performance manage one of my team, but I don't want to overwhelm them. Can I share some examples of issues with you and get your advice on how to approach them?"

If you are able to collaborate with your mentor on a project, that's even better, because there will be project-specific examples you can use for coaching, after which they can see you in action and provide real-time feedback. If not, then the above topics should give you enough to get through a year of sessions with that individual. Obviously, you can determine your own topics based on what is happening within the company or your team, but these are ideas to get you started with meaningful coaching and conversation.

My client Maria hated networking. Not only was it her least favorite thing to do, but she was also positioned within a company where it wasn't very feasible for her to meet people in other divisions. Our first few sessions were met with a lot of resistance to networking (unsurprisingly) citing the various reasons why it wouldn't work, only for me to wear her down over time.

During a season of extreme change in her organization, people were not hiring, and she was very frustrated with the lack of mobility and growth. She had all of the skills and abilities of a director but was struggling to get the opportunity to showcase them in her current team, so she decided to look externally. Meanwhile, I was pushing her to expand her network within the firm and connect with people in new ways.

As with all things, when it rains it pours. One of Maria's external conversations escalated rapidly into a director-level job offer managing a similar product for a competitor. Simultaneously, what she had assumed was a simple coffee chat with a woman in another part of the organization turned into a formal interview for that woman's replacement position. Within weeks, she had two job offers and a decision to make.

I share this example in case you are also feeling extreme resistance to this exercise; many people do. It is uncomfortable and sometimes frightening to put yourself in a position to have to advocate for yourself, let alone with a complete stranger. But it is well worth the effort and temporary discomfort. The worst thing to many in an interview process is to hear, "We think you're great, but we already had someone in mind within the organization." This can easily be avoided by strategic and intentional networking.

Assuming that now you have a robust network established, how do you 'warm it up?' A 'warm network' is a group of people that you could reach out to who would be unsurprised to hear from you. Warming up your network happens progressively over time and with strategy in mind.

If you have maintained your quarterly meetings outlined above, then those individuals would be considered warm already. But with all these things, life gets busy and in the way. If those quarterly meetings have dropped off, we want to bring them back and increase their frequency to every other month for the individuals who work within areas of the business you would like to move to in the future. For your two-times-per-year individuals, we want to meet with them in the next 30 days to re-establish connection and ensure their advocacy for you, were you to apply for a promotion or new position internally.

Warming up these relationships prepares them to think positively about you if asked for a reference or an attestation to your abilities or character. It also ensures that if these individuals were to open a new position, you would be a candidate that they have in mind. This is a much easier hill to climb than applying cold to a position within your organization without any pre-existing relationships.

Lastly, let's discuss maintaining external relationships and networks. No doubt you've had some good bosses and some bad ones. For the latter, do not feel the need to maintain that relationship once you escape (maybe escape is an extreme word, but it probably felt that way when you landed a new job). For the former, if you have a good relationship with that individual, I highly recommend putting them on your one-to-two-times-per-year list.

My first boss out of college and I still talk once or twice a year to this day, even though I worked for him over 13 years ago. Our relationship was strong and our ways of approaching problem-solving were so similar that I knew we would cross paths again, making it valuable, and honestly enjoyable, to maintain a relationship. There are a handful of leaders like this over the course of my career who I intentionally keep in touch with (some were direct supervisors and others were mentors).

When starting to look for external opportunities, it is important to also warm up these relationships. Reach out to individuals within your network, schedule a call to understand what they are doing now and to share your own journey. Even if you don't want to work for their company specifically, they are likely to have connections elsewhere that they can refer you to. These referrals and recommendations are key to propelling your career forward and helping you build the career path that you want.

This creation and maintenance of relationships with peers and leaders will allow you to build momentum towards future opportunities. However, with every individual we resonate with, there will be more with whom we struggle to establish connection. These disconnects can lead to frustration and conflict as we aim to progress our careers.

CHAPTER 9

Interpersonal Conflict and How to Disagree

con·flict

/Kan flik(t)/ noun

A serious disagreement or argument

"YOU CAN'T BE honest at work. People who provide feedback or try to make things better end up on a 'list' and get fired." This is a widespread belief. I see it spread all over social media and hear it on almost every call with clients. I've felt this way about certain organizations I've worked for. I've gotten feedback that I am too direct and too honest and that it would hamper my progression. Long story short: I've been there.

The reality is that this is a lie. It is a palatable and easy to digest lie that we tell ourselves when we struggle to communicate effectively. We hide behind the 'fact' that we were right rather than take ownership for our tone, language, and communication skills in a way that sets us up for success in the long term. But unfortunately for us, being right does not outweigh collaborative communication.

Secret #21: How you communicate your disagreement is more important than your opinion

Most of us have sat in a meeting and said, "That won't work?" or, "This way makes more sense." Or even, "You don't understand." It can be hard when you see a clear solution to a problem and feel that the organization or your leadership won't listen. However, it is likely that you lack clarity around leadership's goals and context, ultimately setting you up for failure if you feel that everyone is against you.

There are three things I commonly see happen in these scenarios that lead to a breakdown in communication:

Your leadership does not always want the most direct solution

Saying that workplace politics does not exist would be dishonest. In fact, politics gets more present and more difficult to navigate at more senior levels of leadership. This means that sometimes when solving or addressing a problem, leadership is also navigating politics at a senior level that you are not privy to.

This could mean that while your solution may be the right one, it requires collaboration with an area that is unwilling to support. Alternatively, it could mean that while your solution may be the right one, leadership is making a play for more scope and your solution does not provide that opportunity. It could also mean that while your solution is the right one, it costs too much given the state of the organization.

Your leadership may have context that you do not have visibility into

Most people are intrinsically self-absorbed and focused on their own priorities. This isn't necessarily a bad thing, but in the workplace environment it is easy to get tunnel vision, where your priorities eclipse those of the larger company.

This means that while your solution might fix *your* problem, it may also create issues elsewhere in the organization. It can also mean that while your solution may resolve your problem, it may be insensitive to needs of the broader organization that could be solved at the same time. Lastly, it means that when presented with the problem, you may be putting it into the context of your position and missing the larger goal.

You are not effectively bringing people along on the mental journey you have experienced

Some people are natural problem-solvers. They see an issue and their brain jumps straight to tactical mode to resolve it as quickly and efficiently as possible. Some people are highly analytical. They see data and can easily draw conclusions and apply them to make directional decisions for their business.

What a great skill, right? Unfortunately for these individuals, what can seem so obvious to them given their experience, knowledge, and acumen is not obvious to their counterparts and leadership. As a result, their solution jumps so far ahead of where the rest of the room is at mentally that it can lose its impact.

Any of these reasons could create opposition for your idea from those who need to buy in for your success. This slows things down and ultimately can make leadership decide to go in a different direction. That is why learning to navigate these disagreements is key to your progression.

Note that while this chapter is put into the context of

disagreeing on a proposal or solution, the tools and tips presented can be applied to disagreements of all types including personality mismatches, communication styles, leadership styles, people management, and more.

So how do you de-escalate and resolve conflict? There are certain tools you can apply to help you be more successful, but everything starts with understanding the type of people you are working with.

Learn the type of person you're disagreeing with

I categorize my colleagues into one of two very broad categories and then tailor my communication from there.

1: The King

- Everyone exists to serve the King—this individual only works with you when they need something, and they treat everyone as if they work for them.
- Your purpose on the project or initiative must make their life easier—they will not sign up to take on additional work if they don't feel it benefits them or their team in some way.
- Support, support, support—the key to the King is that you are supporting them rather than the other way around.

Here are some key phrases to use when addressing the King:

- "I'm really here to help you be successful. Can you help me understand exactly what you need so that I can get it done for you?"
- "This project requires many groups to come together. Can you tell me exactly what your goals and measurements for success are so that I can deliver on them?"
- "If you can get me [X] data, then I can make sure to get [Y] done, which will help you and your team."

2: The Specialist

- The Specialist knows *everything*—even if they don't. They feel as though they are the smartest person in the room and decisions made without their involvement are destined to fail.
- Your purpose on the project must defer to their knowledge and expertise—it doesn't matter if you are the SME or the project lead, in the end your key to success is inclusion of the Specialist.
- Defer, defer, defer—when in doubt (and sometimes even when you are not in doubt) defer to the Specialist's knowledge before proceeding.

Here's what to say to win over the Specialist:

- "Obviously, you have a ton of great knowledge. Can you talk me through why you think that this solution wouldn't work?"
- "I think that [X] makes sense. Can you confirm since you are the closest to that particular work?"
- "You have a lot of contextual knowledge here, is there anything that I'm missing?"

It is important to say that neither of these personalities are inherently bad nor that one is better than the other. Only that individuals tend to prefer one of these types of relationships over the other. Understanding the personality categories of the individuals around you can set you up for success when dealing with those people and help you improve your language when you disagree or partner together.

While these approaches may seem obvious, many people do not use or apply them well in practice. Personally, I am a Specialist, so the points under that category resonate the most with me. Even as a senior leader, I see myself more as a source of knowledge and solutions than as a King, and prefer when people do pre-reads with me to get my buy in, rather than pitching an idea in a large group (another great tip when dealing with a Specialist).

Secret #22: Catering your communication to the individual will prevent conflict and disagreements before they arise

Not exactly rocket science, I know, but think about the people in your organization who can be difficult to work with and to get buy-in from. If they are a Specialist, would a pre-read where you deferred to their knowledge be helpful to mitigate disagreements in a broader meeting? If they are a King, is there a way to position your proposal as a way to help their team get what they want or need? When you think about your stakeholders in advance and prepare for that communication, you increase your chances of success and decrease the amount of conflict you have to navigate on the back end.

Practice *nemawashi*

The Japanese have a word that applies here: *nemawashi*. This literally translates as 'turning the roots' but is a colloquialism for 'decisions happen in the hallways.' It is the informal business process of layering the foundation for a proposed change or project by talking to the people concerned and gathering support informally (i.e., in the hallway) before making a formal proposal.

This is a process which will greatly increase your chances of success. When you apply the rules for networking from Chapter 8 with this philosophy of pre-reads and specific communication, you will see your career propel forward. If the first time your boss or your leadership team hears of your great idea is in a big formal meeting with 20 participants, your chances of success are minimal.

Instead do the pre-work and dramatically increase your chances.

So what do you do if you face opposition or disagreements in those sessions? You apply the following five tips for conflict resolution:

1. Ask a ton of questions: Most opposition can be phrased as a question that allows the other person to justify their position without becoming defensive. Learning to phrase your feedback as questions empowers the other person to bring you along with them and saves you potential embarrassment if they are right. Here are some examples:
   a. Rather than say, "That won't work," say, "Can you help me understand how that would work in this situation?"
   b. Rather than say, "You don't understand," say, "Have you discussed this solution with [X] team? I want to be sure that this meets their needs as well."
   c. Rather than say, "[X] would work better," say, "Have you considered [X] alternative solution? I want to be sure we've evaluated all options."
2. Acknowledge and then respond: This was the number one tip that changed the trajectory of my career (I truly feel it should be taught in colleges across the world). When presenting a solution or reviewing a proposal from others, we can naturally become defensive of our work or perspective. This causes us to jump straight to our responses rather than appreciating collaboration. The easiest way to change this is to acknowledge first before you respond. When someone proposes an alternate solution, start with, "Thank you so much for bringing that up," before jumping into why it won't work or that you already thought about it. When someone asks you a question, say, "That is a great question," before talking about why it isn't applicable. This small change in behavior will make others feel included and collaborative rather than discouraged or discounted.
3. Disagree without saying no: Sharing your concerns rather than disagreeing outright is more of an art than a science. One of the easiest ways to implement this is to say, "I understand why we would want to do this [acknowledge before you respond] but I do have a few concerns..." and share those thoughts. A non-toxic

work environment is open to hearing risks and concerns, even if they ultimately decide against heeding them.

4. Bring people on your mental journey: As mentioned earlier in this chapter, when you easily see a solution to a problem, it is common to quickly jump too far ahead of the rest of the group. Learning to bring people along on your mental journey is a skill that prevents high performers from getting too frustrated and losing their audience. When in a meeting with a larger audience (think more than three other participants), it is key to ensure everyone is tracking your thought process. This is done by implementing the following steps (which I refer to as RASI for short).

   R—Restating the problem/qualifying the ideal outcome: This ensures everyone is on the same page with what is trying to be done.
   A—Asking qualifying questions: About the data, process, proposal, or outcomes to drive everyone to the same solution.
   S—Stating your solution: What is going to solve those questions and meet that need?
   I—Including others for buy in: Ask the Specialist to weigh in or validate that this meets the King's needs. Ensure there is an accord across the group before progressing into the tactical 'how' of implementation.

5. Everything is a yes: There is nothing you can be asked to do that you cannot do with enough people, time, or money. While this is more applicable at the senior manager level or higher, it is a good practice to apply to your career at all stages. When upholding your boundaries, everything can be done; it just requires a trade-off of priorities, more people, more time, or more money for systems, consultants, or professional services. When you can clearly articulate the cost of projects in these terms, it empowers your leadership to make wise decisions and keeps you from having to disagree in the first place. In the end, they are the boss, and they can decide how best to use their resources (i.e., you).

Once you master and apply these five tips, you will find that conflicts de-escalate rapidly. You may also find yourself being more productive and getting the results you need with less stress or discomfort. *But* you may find that in the end, leadership still wants to go in a particular direction that you disagree with.

Once you understand that, you learn the next secret.

Secret #23: You are not always going to get your way

When you don't get your own way, it is important to apply the 'disagree and commit' practice. First coined by Amazon in the early 2000s and later scaled across multiple companies (specifically in big tech) the practice of disagreeing early and ultimately committing to leadership's vision requires letting go of our pride for the sake of the broader team's success.

Accept that some of your best ideas will be rejected

We all think that we have the best ideas and that we know what is best for our team and organization, but sometimes leadership takes things in a different direction. When this happens, you can absolutely apply the five tips above, but if they still decide a different direction you need to let it go and start working. In the end, it isn't your company. It's probably not even your department. Arguing until you are blue in the face won't help you be successful or your team get the credit they deserve for their hard work. Instead, apply yourself to making the project as successful as possible (preferably without snide comments or 'I told you so's).

This can be more challenging when the leader of the project or solution is someone you dislike. I've talked before about personality conflicts, but sometimes our dislike of a team member or partner can go deeper than that. It can be challenging to get on board with someone we believe to be incompetent or lazy. This leads to us reacting emotionally and with volatility rather than keeping the long-term goals we have for ourselves and our teams in mind. In order to prevent these unhealthy reactions at work, we must first understand our workplace triggers and how to navigate them. This will help us master interpersonal conflict.

Almost everybody has complained about a coworker at some point. I certainly have. Every day that we go into work, we have a built-in set of expectations for ourselves that we project onto the others around us. A sense of punctuality, organization, ownership, or even base knowledge that we expect of ourselves and of others in turn. These unacknowledged or even unrealized expectations set us up for interpersonal conflict and disagreements.

First, pull out your 11-List from Chapter 4. Look back over the list of things you don't want to be known for at work. This is also a list of traits you will find triggering in the people you work with. We project our own expectations onto those around us, without clearly communicating those expectations. This sets us all up for frustrations or even failure, making it increasingly important for us to understand what is driving us towards unhealthy relationships at work.

When you understand these triggers, you can begin to understand why that one coworker (and yes, we all have at least one) really bothers you more than others. They likely tick off one (or multiple) things you don't want to be and yet are seen across the organization as successful or a leader. This causes us to become increasingly frustrated, short in our communication, and difficult to work with when partnered.

When you know you will be working with this person, prepare ahead of time. Now you know why they bother you, how can you come to peace with their performance or more clearly express your expectations to them so that you can move forward? Are there certain things you know you will want to say that you can rephrase? Set yourself up for success and mitigate issues ahead of time; sometimes doing five minutes of work ahead of a meeting can make the difference between frustration and success.

This issue can be exacerbated for high performers. Because they naturally (or through immense hard work and intention) produce a lot for the company and are able to execute their jobs with ease, they expect everyone around them to do the same. While I believe everyone is capable of being a high performer with enough intention and work ethic, many people have no desire to be at the top of a bell curve. Instead, they are fine sitting in the middle of the pack, delivering their work, and logging off at a decent time. And that is okay!

But the traditional high performer cannot relate or understand that approach to work. Their brains simply aren't wired to look at work as an exchange for a paycheck rather than a manifestation of who they are (something that could fill another book in itself). This makes it incredibly challenging to work with a high performer—and for high performers to work with other partners.

If you are a high performer, you probably think along the lines of, "Fine, I'll just do it myself," a fair amount. You learn not to rely on others and get frustrated when people struggle to follow your mental journey. While you may be successful with this approach as a more junior contributor, you will rapidly start to fail as your role requires more cross-collaboration or managing a team.

You must learn to understand your triggers (whether they are laziness, being slow to get things done, bad communication, or other things) in order to master them. This will become increasingly important when you go on to manage a team. Expecting that every person who works for you will be a high performer is just unrealistic. Not to mention, you will need people in your team who are content to complete BAU work and aren't striving for promotion. Learning to manage all of these types of employees is key to your success and progression over the long term.

CHAPTER 10

Managing Vs Leading

managing

/manijiNG/ adjective

having executive or supervisory control or authority.

Regardless of whether or not you are currently managing a team, this chapter is critical to your career progression. While this is not a management or a leadership book, I would be remiss if I didn't touch on these necessary skills for long-term success. The fastest way to propel your career forward is to enter into, and excel at, management. This is why so many people end up in the management track, even if it isn't a good fit for their skills (more about this in the next chapter).

As your career grows and develops using the secrets and strategies from the previous chapters, you will undoubtedly be asked to manage a team at some point. Likely, you will be given very few (if any) resources with which to learn the relevant skills, and you will be burdened not only by your own continued development but also by the development of your new team. We've already learned that on average managers receive their first management training 11 years after they begin to manage people. When I first heard that statistic, I was shocked. Employees are thrown into management positions, and no one tells them what to do for over a decade? No wonder so many bosses are terrible. But don't worry—you won't be.

The goal here is to equip you with the skills that you need in order to step into a management role successfully and with a high level of business acumen regardless of what your company provides to prepare you. We will talk through tactical steps that will help you find greater success in your team while ensuring your self-advocacy doesn't deplete when you move to a team-focused attitude. We want to enhance your existing skillset rather than replace the knowledge that you've built over the course of your career.

It is important to acknowledge that the skills required to effectively manage and lead people are very different from those required of individual contributors, which is why so many high-performing individual contributors struggle to manage teams once they are promoted. They drop in performance dramatically, and without any support they flounder and eventually fail. Luckily for you, I am going to unveil some of the secrets of leadership that will set you up for success when the time comes.

Secret #24: Managing and leading are not the same

Although the terms are often used interchangeably in the workplace, in reality the functions of managers and leaders are very different. Many managers know how to manage but not how to lead; we call these individuals 'micro-managers.' There are just as many leaders who don't know how to manage: the world calls them 'absent bosses.' It is rare to find yourself in the ideal position of working for a boss who knows how to both lead and manage. It is even rarer to become such a leader yourself.

This is why I feel the jump from senior manager to director is one of the most challenging across all industries and job types. No matter how successful you are at the senior manager level, you cannot make the jump to director without being able to lead. Both skillsets might be different, but they are equally important to your long-term success.

Managing is about being able to oversee a group and ensure their tasks are completed on time and with a high level of accuracy, whereas leading requires the ability to create a long-term vision for organizational success and then understand how your team fits into that vision. These may sound somewhat similar in that they both relate to direct supervision of individuals, but one takes a targeted short-term view, while the other requires a long-term strategic vision.

In order to build both skills, we will start first with management.

Understand the three pillars of effective management

Effective management requires only three things:

1. being able to set clear expectations for your team members,
2. regular check-ins for development and project completion,
3. a keen understanding of the learning styles and goals of your individual team members.

If you can master these three things you will be better than 90% of managers out there.

Setting clear expectations

The biggest mistake I see new managers make is that they expect their team members to have all of the business-specific knowledge and context that they have, when in reality if the team could all operate independently at the manager's level there would be no need for a manager. Your primary job as a manager is to set clear expectations and give good context to your team.

Here is an easy acronym to help you as you begin to do this: CODS.

C—Context: First set the context of your ask. Are you trying to answer a specific question? Is this an efficiency gain? Is it a request from a stakeholder? Does this help a project stay on track? Does it provide detail for a budget? Ultimately, why do you need this information or output?

O—Outcome: Second is to outline (roughly) the output you are requesting. As your team members get more senior, you can provide more freedom in this step, allowing them to problem-solve as they see fit and iterate with you as they progress, but for more junior team members you want to be specific with what you expect to see. Is it a pivot table summarizing the data? A dashboard? A slide deck? A recap email? Set some expectations about what they should ultimately deliver to save you both time. Even as a director, my C-suite would often outline a shell slide deck, report output, or dashboard request list to help me and my team understand exactly what they were looking for. Providing output guidance does not limit the abilities of the do-er, but it provides a higher chance of probability that their ultimate deliverable will be correct.

D—Deadline: When is this due? Do you want to see a first draft by the end of the day, second by end of next week, and final on the 15th? Does the final need to be submitted before a big meeting? This is a great step to not only set delivery expectations for you and the person completing the work, but also to set checkpoints for project progress in between the start of the work and the final delivery date.

S—Source: Where can they get more information and data, or ask questions related to this work? Sometimes the source is ourselves; we have the deep-set knowledge on the request and where to access various related data sets. But other times, we may be directing them to a peer or another team that has more information related to the work that they can partner with on their final product. If you do not direct them to where they can find more information, they will either operate with limited information and deliver a subpar product or they will come to you constantly with questions you don't have time or information to support, leaving the product (you guessed it) subpar.

I find that this acronym can be beneficial not only to the employee who is being assigned the work, but also for the manager. It forces us to assess the feasibility of the work we are requesting, give some thought to how we might execute, and set up a reasonable time frame for completion. It also empowers the employee to prioritize their work, assess if they can realistically deliver in that time period, and ask the questions they need in order to deliver.

Secret #25: Success starts at assignment, not at completion

If you set your team up for success when you assign the work to them, rather than trying to create success after the work is done, you will be more effective. This is true in both the expectation-setting outlined recently and in how you advocate for yourself and your team. When your team starts working on a project, you should be helping them understand how that work ties into the greater team strategy (more on this later in the chapter) as well as what impact it will have on the company.

Conduct management ceremonies

It is important to your success as a manager and to your team's success to have good ceremonies and meetings in place that allow updates to happen organically. You need to set up time to develop your team, just as you are setting up time to further your own career. The structure that I like to place with my team is as follows:

- Bi-weekly one-on-ones to discuss priorities, real time feedback, and any escalations or roadblocks. I assign ten minutes to each of the three topics (totaling 30 minutes) and let my team members lead sections one and three, while I lead section two—providing feedback on their performance.

- Alternating bi-weekly team meetings with the entire group for each person to share personal updates, project successes, and context with the full team. I kick these off with high priorities from leadership and context they may need and then hand it off to the team to lead their own updates. These sessions will generally run for an hour.
- In January I hold a goal-setting call with each individual and discuss what they need to focus on in the upcoming 12 months to achieve their goals. This is inclusive of soft skills and technical skills and includes career progression conversations.
- A mid-year review takes place in June to ensure employees are tracking to their goals, provide long-term career progression advice and guidance as well as brand alignment and creation.
- In October and November I conduct year-end-review prep to ensure goal completion is articulated well in formal year-end reviews and that team members are not surprised going into formal evaluations.

Talk to your team constantly to ensure that their expectations of their performance are aligned with yours. This prevents disappointment when year-end evaluations are completed and fosters clear communication between manager and employee.

This can be more challenging where an employee is underperforming and requires constructive feedback, which brings us to the next secret.

Secret #26: A successful employee begets a successful leader

Too often I see managers who are afraid of sharing the glory with their team members for fear that the employee will garner a more favorable opinion than the leader. This is just flat out untrue. Managers who hold this belief will undoubtably build toxic, non-progressive teams that stagnate and eventually fail. Your goal as a manager should be to constantly replace yourself.

Managers struggle with this mentality when they fear that by teaching their team all of their skills, they will ultimately become superfluous and be replaced by the company. The only reason that this would happen is if the manager completely stops their own personal development and self-advocacy. If you continue to follow the strategies of this book while you are a manager, then upskilling your team can only result in you taking on more advanced, interesting, and strategic work for your company in exchange. In short: As your team does better, so too do you for your company.

But this requires intention. Your team will not spontaneously learn your skills through diffusion or even through great opportunity. Your team needs you to personally develop them and provide them opportunities that align with their goals to find progression. This is where management ceremonies become important.

Build an advocacy plan for your team

Once you understand the impact being created by your team, it is your job as the manager to build an advocacy plan. This will be similar to the self-advocacy we discussed in Chapter 5 but targeted more broadly at your entire team. Start by mapping out your team's functional organizational hierarchy—this will describe the high-level work and scope that each team member is responsible for as well as reporting structure of within the team. Then align components of your strategy or 'stretch opportunities' to each individual. Lastly, map the specific projects to that person.

This will help you create brands for each individual within your team. Maybe one team member is focused on automation and efficiency, or is an up-and-coming leader focused on expanding the skills of your team. Maybe they are the communication specialist who is on point for executive leadership communications, or they oversee special projects that support the wider organization. Understand the best skills and areas of impact of your people and then partner with that individual to tie that to their personal brands (outlined in Chapters 3 and 4). If the individuals in your team have not been focused on intentionally building their personal brands, guide them through the aforementioned exercise and support them in communicating that brand vertically up the chain.

As a manager, this work will empower you to talk to your leadership team about what your team is achieving in a way that both highlights your leadership skills as well as the individual specialties and brands of those who report to you. You will feel more ready to discuss the efforts of your team in leadership meetings as well as provide your employees the platform to present their successes themselves.

You will then start what I like to call a 'project roadshow.' The objective of this effort is to tease the work your team is doing to aligned stakeholders while gathering their input. If it is a large enough effort, this may include setting up monthly steering committees with stakeholders to review progress and get feedback. If it is a smaller effort, this might be circulating the work to ensure there is no duplication and set up your team member for success upon completion. Ultimately, you want to start to build excitement for the work that is being done ahead of its final completion.

Once the work is complete to your expectations, bring your employee on the roadshow with you to present their work, speak to the impact, and get final feedback from stakeholders. This will bring you full circle in your expectation-setting, with a final delivery that meets the needs of your organization. It will also give your team member an opportunity to shine and ensure that they know they have your support in future assignments.

Secret #27: Negative patterns are more problematic than negative people

Have you ever had a manager who constantly pointed out your flaws? Every meeting with them was enough to incite anxiety and stress because their mercurial nature ensured you never knew what was going to upset them that day? I have, and it was exhausting. It can be detrimental to your psyche, work ethic, and overall productivity if you feel like everything you do is never good enough.

On the flipside, it is never okay for a manager to let an underperforming employee continue with negative behavior without feedback or consequence. Acclaimed businesswoman and *Shark Tank* veteran Barbara Corcoran explained in an interview why she loves firing employees of this type: "I picked out individuals who were negative, and my attitude toward the negative person was, they were ruining my good kids, because people who are negative have to have somebody else to be negative with them."

By leaving poor performers or negative employees in your team's ecosystem, you are condemning it to failure. So how do you find a balance between the manager who rips everyone apart and an apathetic leader that lets its team destroy itself from the inside?

Manage the patterns, not the person

Simple: You manage the pattern, not the person. What does this mean? As a manager (veering into leadership territory) you need to be able to identify patterns in behavior rather than merely symptoms. Similar to a doctor assessing a range of medical symptoms to identify the disease that causes them, managers must perform a similar assessment of the performance of their employees and address the root-cause behavior patterns with medicine.

Some of the most common 'diseases' that I see in employees, along with some of their symptoms, are:

- Poor attention to detail: small mistakes in their reports or outputs, typos in emails, wrong individuals CCed on communications, misses small deadlines but delivers the overall project.
- Lack of proactivity: waits for clear and step-by-step instructions to complete any work, great at BAU repeatable tasks but struggles to take on new projects or initiatives, doesn't ask any questions and then waits for follow up for any requests.
- Inability to plan and strategize: takes on too much work without clarity of prioritization and then fails to deliver on all of it, doesn't have a clear roadmap to deliver projects and so they are often delayed or incomplete, has great ideas but no follow-through.
- Substandard organization and documentation: doesn't write things down or organize their work so they are often doing multiple things but without significant value, has a plan to do things but no follow-through, communication is scattered and unclear.
- Weak in communication skills and executive presence: does great work but struggles to articulate it well, shy and unspoken in front of senior leaders, unclear or unorganized communication, doesn't know how to tell a story or engage listeners.
- Refusal to delegate: delivers great work and on every workstream, doesn't trust others to do their parts, takes credit and/or work from others on the team.

These patterns of behavior require feedback and management. You can tie multiple issues and areas of improvement to one pattern and then treat the actual disease. It is also much less overwhelming for the team member to receive consistent feedback on 'delegation' rather than what feels like hundreds of disparate pieces of personal feedback they don't know how to fix.

As a manager, by pinpointing the underlying issue you can also provide clear, direct, and consistent feedback to your team members, which will help them stay motivated and engaged rather than beaten down. It will also help you help them solve the problem as you can come up with a plan, tips, and tricks to resolve the issue rather than giving feedback on historical misses that cannot be solved.

How your employees work with you to address these patterns will indicate whether they are 'self-driven' or 'managed employee' types. Employees who exhibit the last two patterns (underperformance in areas of communication and delegation) tend to be self-driven. They will work hard to get their work done, on time, and with a thoroughness to be commended, but they need support in upskilling to more senior levels of leadership. They require less direct management and more direction towards a vision and a goal.

The other four patterns will generally be what I call managed employees. These are the types of employees that require a little more attention and direct management. For these employees, it would be wise to set up more frequent touchpoints on projects and deliverables to ensure that they are making the necessary progress and efforts to combat their patterns. When setting your expectations for work (remember our CODS) your deadlines should include no fewer than two touch points on all deliverables until they start to display better ownership of their work.

Regardless of their pattern and employee type, you as a leader should set an internal goal for when their behavior should have improved, to what level, and how it will be measured. Otherwise, it is easy to fall into the trap of 'working with them to improve' forever. Some companies do this formally on a PIP (performance improvement plan) but I prefer to have these conversations in their one-on-ones, send email recaps with timelines, and be clear on what I need to see. (PIPs tend to make employees feel like they are on the verge of being fired—while this may be true, a discouraged employee will certainly show no progress.) This timeline will help you stay a Barbara Corcoran and not slip into becoming an apathetic manager.

Secret #28: You can't compensate for your team

Every team I have ever taken over and managed has started with a mass exodus from the previous leader. No, it is not because I am an ice queen determined to fire people at every opportunity, but rather I find that when I am brought into an organization to drive forward change (as aligns with my personal brand), most employees find that the subpar work they were delivering under my predecessor will no longer be sufficient. They tend to leave of their own volition.

I have also been told by many leaders when I step into a role, "You won't want to give projects to [employee X]." Or "Keep a close eye on [employee Y]." These managers made the key mistake of compensating for their team rather than managing it. When you decide that it is easier to do all of the work yourself than it is to coach and manage your team, you will instantly stop your own progression.

Build your team up with growth in mind

There are three key factors to keep in mind when you create, establish, or grow your team.

1. Don't be afraid to manage out underperformers: Set clear expectations, give the individuals time to acclimate and deliver, and then clearly communicate patterns and mistakes for growth. If they respond well, great; they're on track for future growth and continued employment. If not, they need to be on their way out.
2. When hiring new people: Focus on great attitudes, work ethic, and culture fits first with technical skills second. While there are a few exceptions to this (basically anything that requires a master's or doctorate degree), in general hard workers can be taught most skills with a good foundation and a good leader. Then lean into their strengths to assign work that will allow them to shine.

3. Delegate: I cannot emphasize this enough. If you are unable to delegate to your team effectively and manage them through execution, your growth and your team will stagnate. Invest time over the short term to train, coach, and guide your team members towards success. This will save more time in the long run through delegation and scale.

When I took my most recent corporate role, the team I joined was a good one. Great personalities and culture, strong leader, and lots of opportunity for results (my trifecta of success). I was excited by the opportunity and determined to help the team scale into the future with automations and improved processes. Within my first six months on the team, two of the most tenured employees left—one to retire, the other to change job types after completing a graduate degree. I absorbed their roles into my team alongside a third person whose manager warned me of their performance.

Suddenly, I was rebuilding the team from scratch with no SOPs (documented standard operating procedures) or direction—honestly, it's my favorite thing in the world. I hired in a new team with a focus on automation and scale, and then managed out the underperformer. Quickly a team that had an average of seven years tenure, was all less than one year old (in terms of experience). Many were concerned that my presence was driving too abrupt a change, while others were merely watching to see what would happen next.

I'll give you the short version: We saw a 30% increase in productivity with no additional staff, automated three reports that had previously been a full-time person's role, and automated a 14-day process down to less than 48 hours. The team won every award in the firm that year, and one of the team members was promoted.

I share this story not to toot my own horn, but instead to encourage you to manage your team. Don't be afraid to performance manage or fire poor performers. Don't be afraid to start fresh with processes and automation. Don't feel like you have to do things the same way as your predecessor. And most importantly:

Secret #29: Strategy is essential

We've touched on all three requirements of being a good manager and ventured into some ways to transform those skills from management to leadership, but the real way you progress your career from management to leadership comes down to strategy and vision.

Build yourself a strategy

In order to build a strategy and a vision you really only need to do (you guessed it) three things.

1. Understand the goals and objectives of your organization and how your team fits into that larger picture. Most companies publish annual or multi-year goals that the company, shareholders, or board have declared the top priorities. If your company doesn't regularly disseminate that information, your top priority should be getting a copy. Work with your leadership to take those goals all the way down to your team level. For example, with the team I described recently a key goal of the firm was to grow in revenue and business but maintain a flat headcount. That requires automation, streamlining, and process improvement to be possible, so those became some of my personal team goals.
2. Learn 'the rule of threes.' I've used this rule dozens of times in this book already—did you notice? This psychological trick is a common practice in consulting as it is the ideal number of points for an individual to digest in one sitting. More than three is overwhelming, while fewer seems like you didn't thoroughly think through your presentation. When you are creating a strategy, vision, or presentation of any kind, think of how you can collect your goals into three categories for your team members to digest. Continuing with the above example, automation and process improvement were some of my goals. Another was driving improved employee engagement, as that was a primary focus of

my Chief Technology Officer. The last goal was creating more data-driven insights for improved decision-making as the firm scaled. Every initiative the team or I was working on could be bucketed into one of these three goals. When building your strategy, you need to do the same.

3. Think through how your team would function in the future if you had unlimited money and resources. Would your team be structured differently? Would you hire more people? Would you outsource certain tasks to other teams? Would you buy software to help the team operate more efficiently? Once you know what you would do long-term, you can align those tasks with your three goals and write out a multi-year roadmap.

Pulling together this high-level strategy gives your team something to focus on and work towards. They will also understand how their individual projects and work fit within the broader structure and purpose of the team and see the growth opportunities that could exist in the future. This will keep them engaged and motivated and will ensure the team doesn't stagnate.

You can also share this strategy with your leadership to help display your skills and advocate for future promotions for yourself. The most successful leaders I have ever worked with always had a vision for where their team was going and what that meant for each individual, including themselves. Secure your growth by delivering impact across your company.

All of this, of course, runs on the fundamental assumption that you want to be a manager and a leader. The reality is that this is not true for all people, and more importantly, may not align well with your skills or passions. So how do you determine if you want to be a leader? Firstly, you keep reading.

CHAPTER 11

Managing Toxic Workplaces, Mental Load, and Your Boss

Mental Load

/ˈmen(t)l lōd/ noun

the unrecognized responsibility of extra work some members will take on to maintain the group; the invisible, non-tangible tasks involved in maintaining a team.

HAVE YOU EVER met a couple going through a divorce, and one partner says something like, "I was totally shocked. All they had to do was ask for me to help and I would have." And the other partner says, "I was sick of asking, you should just know"?

This is a great example of mental load. While partner #1 was willing to help in a hypothetical situation, they were unwilling to remember what had to be done, plan out a schedule to do that thing, follow up to make sure it got done, and keep track of hundreds of items just like that across the home. Instead, they delegated the mental load to their partner and settled for, "Just tell me what needs to be done."

Meanwhile, partner #2 is keeping track of the dishes, laundry, school schedules, doctor appointments, sporting events, practices, and more while trying to make sure they all get done, reminding partner #1, and (at some point) trying to recharge and relax. Now, I am not a divorce attorney or a marriage counselor, and so I have no opinions on whether or not this couple should be getting divorced, but I can tell you in this example partner #2 is carrying more of the mental load. At some point it becomes less mentally taxing to just complete a task yourself than it does to carry the mental load and have to babysit someone else while *they* complete the task.

So, what does this have to do with work and your career success? I hold the somewhat unpopular opinion that this concept of mental load is actually a better indicator of burnout than the number of hours worked or results on an employee engagement survey (the two most common ways companies try to predict burnout and attrition). Someone working 30–35 hours a week would on the surface have a pretty great work-life balance for a full-time employee, but if they are carrying the mental load for their entire team, constantly following up and checking everyone's work to make sure it's been done correctly, managing many team members or lateral counterparts, a key stakeholder in every major project, and trying to stay sane—their mental load is too high, and they *will* burn out.

Someone working 50 hours per week in a full-time job, but who has a very limited and clearly defined scope made up of repeatable tasks where they have no dependencies on others might actually be carrying a very small mental load (another potential reason for attrition over the long term, but we won't be covering that here). Therefore, the number of hours an individual is working doesn't necessarily indicate burnout, though it is a symptom of carrying a heavy mental load in many cases.

What does this mean for you as a leader and as an individual? Well, that's another secret:

Secret #30: Managing your mental load should take priority over managing your workload

Once you're a leader, this also means that you are responsible for managing the mental load of your team members as well as their capacity. This is more challenging than you might think, especially if you are managing high performers who are especially inclined to take on too much mental load. There are a few ways to gain insight into the mental load of your team members. While some will be vocal about theirs, sharing their stress at taking time off or their anxiety with the workload (both red flags), others will require more investigation on your part—you might need to ask about how they feel when they disconnect from work, their bandwidth for additional projects, and for a list of their current projects.

Be careful that proactivity on your part doesn't become micromanagement of their workload. If you are building trust and open communication in your team (per the last chapter) individuals will ideally tend to bring you their concerns or stresses of their own accord; but do keep an eye on any team members who are likely to silently bite off more than they can chew.

Choose your tactics for reducing mental load

As an individual, you need to understand what tactics for decreasing mental load work best for you and put them into practice. You should also prioritize building a good relationship with your direct supervisor so that you have an avenue for discussing your mental load with them. Here are some potential tactics to help with your mental load.

1. Lists: I am a list maker. I like to write them down, say them out loud, and repeat them until I find them manageable (yes, I am a little neurodivergent). It can be incredibly helpful to break down your large projects and workload into manageable tasks, put them

to a roadmap or assign them to a specific date, and then start completing them and checking them off your list. Where this can be a struggle is with frequently changing priorities or fire drills that derail your plans (more on how to manage these in #3 and #4), but I still encourage you to write them down. Once they are down on paper, see if you can let them go mentally. Not everyone can, but for some, writing things out physically can take them off your mental load.

2. Time/day blocking: There are a ton of books and articles about time blocking, so I won't spend too much time here. The general concept is that you block certain hours of your day for certain types of tasks. While I do believe this is incredibly beneficial, the more senior I have become and the more meetings I have had to sit in, the less I find myself being able to adhere to this. What I have found increasingly more helpful for me and my team is 'day blocking.' There are certain types of work I do on certain days. I block my calendar Monday and Friday afternoons to get caught up on tasks that are due, I work on slides Tuesday mornings, and record content on Sundays. Once my tasks were organized by day, I found it easier to lock in and get more things done quickly—as well as decrease my mental load—because I am not stressing about Tuesday items on a Monday.
3. Prioritization trade-offs/deprioritization: One common mistake, made especially often by more junior employees, is assuming your boss is keeping track of all the things you're doing and balancing your capacity for you. While I believe they should, they generally will not. It is up to you to come to them with a pre-prepared list of priorities, discuss which ones are the most important or have to be done first, and deprioritize tasks out to either later timelines or omit them from your list completely. Once you build a healthy and consistent practice here, your workload (and thus your mental load) should improve. Learn to let go of the deprioritized items to free up mental space to focus on what is important.

4. Delegation (comprehensive): Managing people is not easy. Getting a new person on your team does not mean that you will instantly have someone you can give work to, scaling your capacity. Training and developing resources takes time, ultimately costing you more time, effort, and mental load in the short term to bring them up to speed. However, the ultimate goal is to build up resources to whom you can comprehensively delegate. This means scaling your team to a point where you can give them work without still having to carry the mental load for it. We've all experienced delegation where we assign a task but then end up pulled back into the project because someone else doesn't have the context, knowledge, or ability to complete the work. This is not comprehensive delegation—which requires the other individual to take the work and run with it—therefore it does not decrease the mental load.
5. Creating a strategy: While this may be more common at senior levels, it is beneficial for all levels of management and leadership. When you have a clear strategy and roadmap for the work that you are doing, ratified by your boss or leadership team, it is easier to push back against new priorities (citing that they don't align with the agreed-upon roadmap or that they would delay important roadmap items). This helps you to prioritize, deprioritize, manage your time, and maintain consistent lists of tasks. All of these come together to lighten the mental load and allow you to focus on what is most important.
6. Pro tip for managers: I do not always share a full multi-year roadmap with my team. While this is a common workplace practice, I find that sometimes it can increase mental load by stressing employees out if they think too far in the future about a workload that doesn't exist yet. While my team is always aware of where we are going strategically, we are usually only focused one or two years into the future rather than thinking too long-term and losing sight of our priorities.

Here are some tools that I use to help me stay on top of my workload (these are unsponsored, but I find them incredibly helpful).

- aNote application (iPhone): This allows you to create lists in the note section, folders for different types of lists or notes (I use it for budgeting as well), and create to-do lists. You can even create to-dos in the future on specific days or set tasks to repeat at a certain cadence.
- reMarkable tablet: I've heard mixed reviews on these, but I love mine. I also downloaded a linked annual/weekly calendar from Etsy (I am pretty sure it was about $7) that allows me to create daily to-do lists that tie into the calendar, plan my weeks out in advance, and again assign tasks to certain days in the future.
- Pen and paper: Don't overcomplicate it. For years I used a Moleskine dotted journal to create my to-do lists and track my meetings. It doesn't have to be pricey to be effective.
- Weekly vertical planners: I used daily planners for years (Day Designer was a favorite brand of mine before I got my reMarkable) but recently switched to a weekly vertical with time slots so I can see my whole week at a glance. I still need a place for daily to-do lists, but otherwise this works better to structure my time.

Implementing these various tactics in the workplace implies that you can influence your leadership to lead the way you think that they should and prioritize some of the work (rather than all of it) without being contrary to how they are leading now. This can be very hard to do when a leader's style is very different from our own, but ultimately can help us build our own management, communication, and influencing skills while improving our current working environment. The most common ways that poor management manifests are micromanagement, absent management, and reactive management. Influencing these types of leaders requires understanding the core reason for their behaviors, alleviating concerns where you can, and creating a strong subculture in your own team (we will talk more about this in Chapter 12).

No matter how great you are at communicating, everyone at some point in their career experiences a bad boss—it is the number one reason people quit their jobs. A bad boss requires a very different type of skill: managing up. This is the art of influencing your manager in such a way that they—and by extension you—succeed despite their shortcomings. Managing up gets a very bad reputation, as we assume that leaders are all trained when they step into management roles and that they should be able to effectively lead a group.

One of the easiest ways to manage up is introducing optionality to offset mental load. Optionality ultimately comes down to lightening the load for your boss. If you assume that whatever your mental load is, your boss is carrying that much for each of their direct reports plus their own burden (minus the comprehensive delegation they are able to do), you can see why we would want to prevent adding to that as much as possible. This means that when you are advocating for yourself, attempting to prioritize workloads, or proposing a new project/solution, we want to do as much thinking as possible up front for your leadership.

- When requesting a raise, research market rates and create a presentation or document that outlines your value, this research, and your request (websites like Payscale.com can be very helpful for this exercise).
- When advocating for a promotion, make a one-pager outlining the scope of your role at the next level and highlight the competencies you have that map to that level of seniority.
- When proposing a solution, flush out multiple options for your boss and propose them on a single slide so that they are empowered to make a decision.

By doing this preparation rather than just bringing problems, complaints, and wishes to your boss, you avoid adding to their mental load and increase your chances of getting what you want.

It is important to note here that there is a very large difference between having a bad boss who requires some managing up, or a difficult stakeholder who doesn't always communicate well, and working in a toxic, unhealthy environment. There are plenty of toxic work environments that exist today (unfortunately), and it is important for you to be able to identify when you find yourself in one. Doing so will enable you to save your physical, mental, and emotional health by getting out of a bad situation.

Here are some ways to identify if the role you are in currently is toxic:

- On Sunday nights you find yourself dreading getting up in the morning to go to work.
- You are afraid to ask questions or get clarification for your role, for fear of backlash or yelling.
- You feel in any way discriminated against (whether for your age, sex, orientation, race, religion, or anything else).
- You know you cannot go to your boss for support or help because of politics in the workplace.
- Working extreme overtime without pay, verbal abuse, and/or leadership/subordinate dating are regular occurrences.
- You find yourself taking time off (either paid or unpaid) just to recover from your job.

If any of these ring true for you, my advice is to quit your job. It can be scary and feel unnatural when you have been living in fight or flight for so long, but changing your environment can dramatically change how successful you are. As we talked about in Chapter 3, a mismatch of your skills to the needs of an organization can hold you back from reaching your potential. Coupled with a toxic company culture, it can be detrimental to your confidence, speed of growth, and mental health.

This is our next (not-so) secret.

Secret #31: A toxic workplace isn't good for anyone

You might be thinking, 'But I work with people who seem to love the toxicity and they are rewarded for it.' Yes, some people *can* thrive in a really toxic workplace despite the adverse conditions, but don't try to be one of them. Trying to survive these environments of constant backstabbing, avoiding escalating confrontations, and dreading our work ultimately brings out the worst in us—and surviving the workplace isn't worth sacrificing your humanity. Escape is the best path forward.

Leverage your workplace support networks

1. Human resources: For any documented or egregious toxic behavior (e.g., anything related to your sexual orientation, race, age, or gender), you should follow the advice and recommendations of your HR department. This can mean discussing your situation with an HR business partner or filing an employee relations complaint.
2. Benefits: Lean into the available benefits your company provides. This may include mental health services, LOAs (leave of absence), career coaching services, training/certifications, and more. Work with your benefits team to understand what is available to you and how it can help you overcome your current situation.
3. Unions: If you have a workplace union, you have more support than most. You can generally take your grievances to the union for support and protection against toxic workplace practices.
4. Peer network: Oftentimes toxicity can be a side effect of a single bad leader in an organization. When this is the case, networking your way onto another team within the same company is the fastest and most direct way for you to put yourself in a better position.

So, what do you do if these attempts do not improve your workplace? You leave. You get a new job offer, you turn in your two weeks' notice triumphantly, and you part ways onto greener pastures. What then?

Secret #32: It takes time to recover from a toxic workplace

Just like finding yourself again after a relationship falls apart, it can take time to get back to who you were before joining a toxic workplace.

Between jobs, give yourself time to rebuild your confidence in yourself and in your skills

It's very likely that you've been conditioned to hold your tongue and keep quiet at your recent workplace, so focus particularly on the skills of adding value and contributing to solutions.

Also go back and re-read Chapters 2 through 4. Rediscover your unique skills, brand, and abilities so that you can start to find yourself and your confidence again. Build your brand statement and begin weaving it into conversations.

And lastly, decide what you want for yourself and your career now that you are free from the expectations of your last job. Do you even want to work in the same industry or area of business? Is it time for a change? And long term, do you even want a corner office?

CHAPTER 12

Do You Even Want a Corner Office?

executive

/ ex·ec·u·tive/ noun

a person with senior managerial responsibility in a business organization.

NOT EVERYONE IS destined for a corner office (usually the preferred office for senior executives)—not because of lack of ability, but rather due to a lack of passion for that type of work. Growing up, I always believed that the reason there were so few chief executives was because there were so few companies, but the reality is that most companies will make space at the top for great talent. The problem is that their options are limited when it comes to finding people who have the technical knowledge, soft skills, personality, and drive for executive leadership.

As a result, companies keep their executive teams small, correctly assuming that it is better to have fewer leaders with great skillsets than to bloat the upper levels with subpar talent. Obviously, occasionally people sneak through to the top layers and raise the question 'what were they thinking?' but generally individuals must display a myriad of skills to get the attention and clout necessary to climb to those highest levels.

So, while every skill a CEO possesses can be learned, some people will be more naturally inclined to learn them, while most will not want to dedicate the time and effort it takes.

Secret #33: Most people will never be executives

I know what you're thinking: 'Duh!' We all look around our companies and see that roles get sparser the closer you get to the top. But what I am telling you right now is: If *you* specifically are not an executive already, there's a good chance you never will be. And I know, I know, now you're thinking, 'But I bought this book! I'm following all of your advice! How can I *not* become an executive?' Well, with the skills you've learned along our journey together, it certainly isn't because you aren't good enough to be an executive. No, it's because there's a good chance you're about to discover that you don't even really *want* to be one.

I remember my first interview out of college. I had somehow talked myself into a room with three other candidates and none other than the CFO of the company. He was talking us through the company's direction and current strategy and asked each of us what we thought. The other candidates talked about how brilliant it was, how they couldn't wait to see it be successful, and about how much they wanted to be part of it. He looked at me.

I said, "I don't think you understand your core customer. The plan you just outlined, while it would be brilliant to the right individual, doesn't speak to the existing customer base. You're going to lose a lot of money before you make any unless you can recruit new customers quickly." The room went deadly silent, and the hiring manager laughed. "I told you," he said to the CFO.

While my fellow candidates and I sat in confusion, the CFO sat back slowly in his chair. He looked at me keenly before dismissing the other three candidates. His next question shouldn't have surprised me, but I found myself unprepared: "Where do you want to be in five years?" I thought for a moment. "Maybe not five years, but I want to be sitting in your chair, with your title. Ultimately, I want your job." I shrugged as though the answer was obvious.

He laughed outright and hired me on the spot. There is a lot more to this story, but I became essentially an internal consultant for the CFO from that day forward, solving the problems he didn't have time for, creating reports he didn't know he needed, and understanding the company from the bottom to the top. It was the most amazing learning experience I could've asked for.

My answer in that room was aspirational and probably far-fetched, but I knew early on what I am about to teach you—there is nothing a CFO or CEO or COO knows that you cannot learn. The challenge is that you have to work hard to get that knowledge, understand it, and apply it. Throughout this book I have taught you secrets that took me 15 years to learn, already saving you time and helping you get a leg up on the competition. But the reality is that most of the people who read this book (90% according to most studies) will read, appreciate, and then immediately disregard these lessons.

We are creatures of habit and comfort. We like to do things our way and without feeling uncomfortable. It is why so many people struggle with putting themselves out there to network, as we covered in Chapter 8, despite it being proven repeatedly to be the biggest differentiator in most people's careers. The issue is that being an executive is comfortable for very few people. It requires getting outside of your comfort zone constantly to make decisions regarding topics of which you have limited—at best—knowledge and context.

If you want to be an executive, prepare to leave your comfort zone behind

If all you can think about is how badly you want to become an executive, understand that there are five *non-negotiable* skills and attributes you need to possess.

1. Public speaking

You must be able to hold an audience's attention and clearly articulate your perspective to large groups at regular occurrences. This also includes being able to answer questions for which you are unprepared or uninformed.

Sorry to all of my introverts out there. You can find immense success in your life without ever speaking publicly, but you cannot and will not find success as an executive. Now before you immediately call me out for my belief that every skill a CEO possesses can be learned, you can in fact learn public speaking.

Famous entrepreneur Steven Bartlett discusses his dislike and fear of public speaking in his book *Diary of a CEO*: "There I stood, frozen, terrified and mute, for one of the longest minutes anyone has ever endured… experiencing what people refer to as 'stage fright'."

This icon, who now travels the world speaking on stage 50 weeks a year in every corner of the globe, started out hating the idea of speaking in front of a group. He would shake, freeze, and run off stage, presumably to breathe into a paper bag, before signing himself up to do it all over again. He understood early on something that it takes many people decades to learn: That being able to speak to a large group, successfully and comfortably, is one of the biggest indicators of career success.

He goes on to discuss the absolute necessity of learning public speaking, the impact it had on his career as a CEO, and the various methods by which he eventually learned this skill that had previously eluded him. He is renowned as a marketing genius, podcast star, and now best-selling author almost exclusively due to his public speaking. He turned what was a weakness into a strength that provided him with the platform for millions of *dollars'* worth of success.

2. Moral Character

You must have a strong moral character and value honesty, diversity of opinion, and trust. CEOs who lack this attribute ultimately cause negative consequences for their organizations, often leading to decreases in revenue and even the total failure of the company.

Do you recognize the name Jeffrey Skilling? Jeff was CEO of Enron during one of the largest, most publicized corporate scandals of all time, one that led to the imprisonment of most of the company's leadership team and ultimately its bankruptcy. I don't know Jeff (I'm just pretending we're on a first-name basis), but I would guess that he didn't get to the CEO level and think to himself 'I'm going to commit accounting fraud, lie to my shareholders, and bankrupt this company.'

What he did do is have a flexible moral character that allowed him to falsify financial documents to shareholders. He was unwilling to listen to the staff members and financial leads who raised concerns over multiple years regarding financial statements and losses, and instead slowly bankrupted his company. He eventually served 24 years in prison for his crimes, and Enron became the poster child for the importance of financial audits.

For you, or anyone else, to be a successful CEO, you must inspire trust and motivation in your employees, and of course, not go to jail. This, combined with increasing attention to morality and diversity of thought across public opinion, is why those without a strong moral character will ultimately fail.

3. Strategy

You have to know how to lead and motivate people (just like we talked about in Chapter 10). You need to see beyond how a company operates today to the future that awaits. You must be a visionary who is able to tie that vision to actionable goals.

If you were alive in the late 1990s or early 2000s (or even if you weren't) you have probably heard of the video rental chain Blockbuster. I remember the excitement of walking into a Blockbuster store, perusing the aisles for my Friday night entertainment, and then picking out my choice of candy from the blue and yellow counter. It was a cultural phenomenon and has since become the peak of nostalgia.

This is because Blockbuster was forced to close all of their stores and declare bankruptcy—oh, how the mighty fall. I expect that business schools and books like mine will talk about Blockbuster for years to come as a case study in poor business practices. But in the end, I believe that they truly only made two mistakes. The first was that they didn't have a clear vision or understand the customer's increasing prioritization of instant gratification (i.e., streaming services), and the second was that they partnered with Enron, of all companies.

If we set aside the second, as we've already discussed it, and focus on the first, Blockbuster was so comfortable in their brick-and-mortar stores that they didn't prepare for a vision of a different future. This is a common pitfall of many leaders who start to see success with a specific business model or operational structure; they are hesitant to look for new ideas or implement change for fear of rocking the boat. And then… they Blockbuster.

On the other hand, around the same time, some up-and-coming founder started a website to resell old college textbooks. I remember listing the books from my freshman classes online to be resold and buying my next semester's books in turn to save money. Everyone thought it was a great, if limited, idea. This new website, Amazon, was being discussed across college campuses.

Now that website is the largest online retailer and marketplace globally, the primary cloud computing software used by corporations, and one of the largest overall companies in the world. While Amazon's original model of selling books worked from 1994 until roughly 2002 when its offerings expanded, new features, products, services, and options have been added in every year of the company's existence. Its founder and leader, Jeff Bezos, avoided the comfortability crisis that afflicts most CEOs of burgeoning companies and instead focused on a strategy and vision that would eventually allow Amazon to become one of the most successful companies in the world.

Your goal, should you choose the path to executive leadership, is to never get too comfortable. Instead, you must always be thinking about your strategy, the next evolution of your role and team, and how you can continue to add value to your leadership, company, and shareholders.

4. The ability to navigate interpersonal conflict

This gets worse the higher you get, because you encounter more people with strong opinions and deep intellect arguing over resources, direction, money, and clout. Navigating difficult personalities can be the biggest challenge a CEO (or anyone in the C-suite) will face.

In one of the first corporate jobs I held, the CEO and CFO hated one another. We're talking complete opposition of thought and contrary objectives. Their meetings often ended with strong language and their teams rushing in opposite directions to avoid the fallout. And this was no secret—everyone knew, from the admin staff to the janitor. And still they worked together for almost two years, until the CEO left the company.

While they were, to my knowledge, always on opposing sides of the table, my CFO had been hand-picked by the CEO. He had skills that the CEO did not and a focus on financials that the CEO desperately needed to rein him in. The two worked together really well in a type of balance formed around their diversity of thought and had a partnership that very few of us understood.

This was only possible because of their ability to navigate interpersonal conflict in an effort to deliver great results for the company. While they may not have seen eye to eye, they were able to communicate effectively with one another and find middle ground where it made sense, ultimately creating a powerful team for the rest of the company to look up to.

When we talk about diversity in the workplace and good communication skills, this is what we mean. You don't have to agree with everyone you work with, or even like them, to work together well, but you do need to be able to navigate people with different priorities and ways of working to deliver on behalf of your organization.

5. Unwavering confidence

You must believe with everything that you are, that your decisions are the right ones and be prepared to defend them if and when something goes wrong. To instill confidence in your people and your organization, you must have confidence in your choices, so that they can have confidence in you.

Steve Jobs, Elon Musk, Jaime Dimon, Jeff Bezos, Bill Gates—I would be shocked if there are many people who don't recognize the names on this list. Some of the most notable and well-known leaders of the current times, these executives took their companies further than most people can imagine and did so with a flare that was picked up by newspapers, television shows, and social media alike. Love them or hate them, these CEOs all have one thing in common: unwavering confidence and belief in their own ability to lead a company well.

You would be hard-pressed to get any of the above individuals to admit they made a mistake, even with copious amounts of data or reference materials. That is not simply because of hubris or power, it is because a facet of their personalities is complete confidence in their own competencies. This is a requirement for leaders who take up the mantle of CEO. While it may not be so firm a requirement for the CFOs and COOs of the world (though I've known a great many who exhibit a similar profile) to give your people and your teams confidence in where you are going, you must display confidence yourself. This will be true at every level of leadership you possess.

If reading through this list leads you to despair of every reaching an executive position, you might be right—but entering the C-suite may not be the best path for you anyway.

Secret #34: The right path for your career is a natural alignment to your skills and interests

A lot of people begin their career hoping to get to the upper levels of executive leadership. When I told that CFO that I wanted his job, I was so confident (in the way only people in their early 20s can be). I knew where I was going with my career and I was going to do anything to get there.

Lucky for me, I am pretty observant, and was able to pick up a lot of executive attributes early on in my career; as a result, I was able to avoid many pitfalls I saw in my peers and began networking and advocating for myself early on. I would also be remiss if I didn't mention that my first group of leaders out of school was amazing. I was treated as a peer by many of my managers and leaders, involved in high-level conversations, and given far more context than most of my colleagues. This definitely gave me a head start when I looked across the organization and ultimately instilled in me my later passion for leadership.

However, if you fast forward eight or nine years in my career, I was offered the very job I had requested in that meeting. I went through seven rounds of interviews, met with the board of investors, completed a case study, and went to lunch with the managing committee. I had proven myself to be financially minded, analytical, a clear people leader, and pretty good with technology strategy. A startup technology company wanted me to lead their product and finance organizations as a CFO.

When I received the job offer, I was initially ecstatic. My goal of becoming a CFO was coming to fruition before I was 30! I couldn't believe it. My hard work paid off. I celebrated with a nice dinner and my husband congratulated me on reaching my goals.

Then I turned it down.

Looking back, this was the best decision I made in my career and is the exact moment where I started to be strategic with my career instead of letting it happen to me. This particular role was not the right fit for several reasons, including that the company did not have work-life balance (and I had just had my first child), the CEO was not a particularly good match for my skills, and they lowballed me claiming I was 'young and unproven' (despite the fact that I was their top candidate and everyone agreed I was the most capable).

My goals and needs had shifted over the course of my career. I no longer wanted to work long hours, I wanted to be home with my family. I also had realized that my skill of solving problems in ambiguity was more impactful in operations and tech than it was in finance. In short, a CFO-ship no longer aligned with who I was or what I could best offer a company.

By realizing this, I was able to turn down my 'dream job' and instead take *the right job*—a hybrid chief of staff/strategy role. I learned a lot, was able to apply my skills to an organization that needed them, and it ultimately led to the best job of my career.

I once heard an executive tell a room full of people that she had an 'accidental career,' and at that time it resonated deeply with me. I didn't have a directly vertical job progression but instead kept following my skills into whatever job allowed me to apply them with the most success. It felt like an accident. But this doesn't mean you should just let your job happen to you (remember Secret # 2?).

Avoid the 'accidental career' trap

The idea you can only move vertically in a company is a lie. In fact, most extremely successful people that I have worked with held jobs in multiple different departments, industries, and seniorities. A CHRO that I know said it was more of a 'job lattice' than it was a 'job ladder' and I love that.

Understand your own skills and differentiation in the job market and then use that information to build a personal brand. Once you know who you are, you can network and advocate yourself into better, more senior, positions that best suit your skills. Don't become a CFO when you should be a COO, and more importantly, don't become a CFO when you should be an operations manager. Not all career progressions should or will lead to 'chief' in your title. Make that choice intentionally, not accidentally.

CHAPTER 13

Ghost Cultures and the Leaders You Hire

Culture

/kəlCHər/ noun: culture

The attitudes and behavior characteristic of a particular social group.

EVERY COMPANY POSSESSES what I term a 'ghost culture.' This is what the CEO believes the company culture to be—what is printed on plaques and posted around buildings, and what HR tells potential new hires during recruitment. It is probably printed on the company's website alongside the mission and vision and quoted in public interviews. Everywhere you turn the company has a carefully crafted image of its own culture, but, in reality, that culture simply doesn't exist.

I know that a great deal of money and time is invested in defining company culture. The cornerstones of the organization, values of the employees, and benefits that attract and retain the right people are clearly defined and put in carefully designed pamphlets for consumption. Countless consulting firms exist only to help with defining these attributes and get paid millions per year to do so. Yet much of the time, these exercises are a farce.

The reality is that the culture most employees experience is the subculture that exists only within their direct team and supervisor. The imagined culture of the overall enterprise might exist at the highest levels of leadership, but seldom trickles down to the average employee. This is because the leaders under that cultural umbrella are responsible for constantly hiring managers who fit that culture and will thus perpetuate it. The further you get from the heads of the culture experience, the harder it is to see that culture and perpetuate it. Sort of like the children's game 'Telephone.'

For the sake of this discussion, it is important to separate *benefits* from *culture*. Benefits exist equally for every employee and can be accessed by everyone; think about healthcare, legal services, 401(k), etc. Meanwhile, culture is something that must be intentionally maintained by the leader in order to be experienced by the employee; think career progression, promotions, open-door communications, and customer focus.

Some benefits claimed by companies are instead aspects of culture. To give one bizarre example, Google in the early 2010s led the way with unique employee 'benefits': cereal bars, scooters, ping pong tables, arcade games, nap pods, and more. Suddenly Google was *the* place to work, touting these amazing benefits as a key reason why. But these are not really benefits at all—they are an aspect of the culture.

If you are working 80-hour work weeks because you are understaffed and overworked, are you taking advantage of the ping pong tables? No. You don't want to spend one minute more at work than you absolutely have to. If your boss yells at you and berates you, are you chilling in a nap pod? No. That would be absurd, and you are instead far more likely to be hiding in a broom closet.

These facilities aren't employee benefits because only a healthy, balanced work culture will allow you to truly take advantage of them. The hostile culture of a toxic work environment will quickly swallow such gestures—you would find them going unused, gathering dust across high-rent floors in your company's building.

Secret #35: Only the culture of your direct manager matters

The way that a manager leads, guides, and coaches their team is the largest indicator of employee satisfaction and retention. This is why so many companies now implement employee satisfaction surveys to measure staff perceptions of the company. Whether large corporations want to admit it or not, the culture within a team is a much better measure of overall company culture and employee experience than the company's tagline.

Get to the truth of your employer company's culture

This is important for two reasons. First, when you are seeking out new employment opportunities or navigating internal corporate change, the way that your direct manager thinks about career progression, team member development, and overall work-life balance is the most important thing you should consider when evaluating the right fit.

This begins with asking targeted questions in the interview focused on your highest priorities within company culture. That could be about employee or business resource groups targeting the support of various diversity groups, mentorship, career progression, feedback and growth opportunities, or internal transfers. Anything that you feel is a high priority to you as an individual and will have an impact on your overall long-term satisfaction with the company. Some of my favorite questions to ask at the end of an interview are:

- "I'm incredibly passionate about mentorship as an individual and a leader. Are there formal programs for mentorship established across the company? Are there any rules or guidelines restricting informal mentorship in the absence of a formal program?"

- "How do you give constructive feedback to the members of your team? What type of support is provided by you and the firm to help individuals turn those opportunities into strengths?"
- "Can you give me three examples of individuals within the team who have either been promoted internally or transferred to other teams across the firm?"
- "I'm excited about the role and how it fits with my skills. Over the long term with this company, I will be looking for opportunities to grow my skills and my seniority level. How often does the organization allow for progression conversations?"
- "What is the average tenure of team members in this immediate team, and what about the organization overall?"
- "What is the thing you dislike the most about the company and this team?"

Many of these questions will help you understand the way that the company and this team operate in more depth than what you can read online or generally will be offered up in an interview.

Another favorite tactic of mine is to request an informal interview with a potential peer on the team. Companies will generally accept this request and pair you with a more senior employee to ask your questions. More often than not, a peer has very little to gain by lying to you, making them a great source of true information. You can ask them the above questions, discuss their personal experience, and make sure you're going to be a good personality fit with not only the hiring manager but also your future peers.

Any objections to this request should be seen as severe red flags. Some companies may claim that this goes against policy, but this is generally a front. Refusal of your request to meet with team members can tell you a few things. The company is either afraid that the team member will tell you bad things that will change your mind; they know they have had too much turnover lately and they don't want that to change your mind; or the team is heavily understaffed and overworked, and they don't want *that* to change your mind.

Sensing a trend? The only reason not to pair you up with a peer in the interview stage is that they are hiding something that will make you not take the job. Just asking to meet with a peer can be a great way to determine the forthrightness of your potential employer and the validity of what the hiring manager is sharing. Figuring out the team's subculture is paramount to long-term satisfaction and short-term success.

The second reason that your company's *true* culture is more important than its cultural tagline: As a manager or leader you have the ability and responsibility to ensure your team has a great subculture. Forget what the ghost culture of your company is. When you become a leader, whether that is managing one person or 100, you have the unique opportunity to create your ideal company culture for your people.

Something that I have found, predictably, always very frustrating is that companies will not teach their employees how cross-calibrations and promotion conversations go. Many employees will work hard all year with a false sense of understanding the company's priorities as well as what will help them achieve their goals. That may be the company policy, but it doesn't have to be yours. I will always explain, in probably too much detail, how year-end scores and promotions are determined so that my team can plan accordingly.

Additionally, as a leader, I have always started every year with a goalsetting exercise. This is not just the standard SMART goals that your company may request, but a tactical deep dive into the following themes:

- "What do you want to get on your year-end evaluation?"
- "Are you looking to get promoted this year?"
- "What soft skills do you need to improve and how can I help?"

This type of goalsetting is generally overlooked, as many managers do not want to overpromise and underdeliver come year end, but I find it incredibly helpful to benchmark employees' expectations early, so that I can cater my feedback throughout the year to those expectations.

Feedback then can look like: "At the start of the year you said you were looking to get a 5 on your year-end evaluation. This project that I am assigning you has the opportunity to make that possible with a high level of execution." Or the reverse: "This mistake pattern is going to hold you back from achieving your goal of a 5 at the end of the year. Behavior needs to change in order to get back on track." I find that while this type of direct communication may be more uncomfortable for me personally, it is incredibly beneficial to the employee who can clearly see how their actions are tied to their goals and whether or not they will achieve them. It also ensures that no one goes into year-end conversations with a big surprise.

This is one aspect of how I create a different subculture within my team compared to the company. It is based on my personal priorities of being a great people leader and developer. I also like to fund lunches on my employees' birthdays, regularly give them high-exposure opportunities to present to executives and leaders across the company, and give half days before every holiday; these things aren't company policy, but if everyone's work can be done or postponed to the following week, I find that it greatly increases team morale.

Some of this is dependent on your leader's culture and how much autonomy you have as a manager, but there is a lot more freedom than most people think. I would rather try to build a great team culture and have my hand slapped, than maintain the status quo and watch great team members leave. This is your burden: With great power comes great responsibility.

As you continue to scale in your journey and become a leader of leaders, this idea of subculture may scale too, but it does not go away. In fact, while you continue to build your own team's subculture, you will also build the clout and reputation to start influencing the overall company culture. This puts you in the position to play your own game of Telephone within your organization and start to expand your subculture (though you may find it more difficult to maintain).

This leads us to the last, but certainly not least, unspoken rule of the career game.

Secret #36: The leaders you hire determine your company culture

I have worked for many executives and senior leaders. Some were amazing, able to articulate the value of their team and advocate for their people, while others were... probably the reason you bought this book. Regardless, they each shaped their own subculture that trickled down into the overall functionality of the group.

Matthew was one such leader. He was brilliant, detail-oriented, and best of all, invested in the success of his team. He cared about each person within his organization and was constantly pushing his upper leadership to invest in employee engagement programs for the betterment of the company.

When he was initially hired, he was walking into an organization with a toxic culture. Complaints filled the annual employee surveys, talks of racism and discrimination of all types permeated manager reviews, and employees were abandoning ship left and right. It was, in short, a cluster.

The first thing Matthew did was clean house. He started at the top, removing all of his direct reports except for one and bringing in people with great culture mindsets and experience. Then, as all subcultures do, that trickled down throughout the organization. Great managers who had suffered under previous leadership rose to the top, shining in a newly restructured organization. Poor managers who had flourished in the toxicity of the previous executives worked their way out quickly to be replaced with high-achieving new hires.

Suddenly, the department that had held one of the lowest employee engagement scores in the company was leading the charge in positive experience. Each leader hired under them more leaders with a similar focus and mindset. A new subculture was born and flourished.

Recruit great leaders

This is why it is so important to hire people with similar values in culture. We will all have different ways of prioritizing work, communicating, and even handling conflict, but culture requires core values alignment in order to be maintained. Studies show that even one bad hire can create a negative experience that impacts the entire organization. To build a high-functioning organization, you must recruit great leaders to lead great teams.

While I might not share Barbara Corcoran's love of firing people, she does make a great point. She goes on to say that one bad apple will poison the rest, spreading negativity, poor work ethic, and a bad attitude. This is especially true with managers. One bad manager can ruin the subculture of a team and bring in a toxicity that is hard to weed out. With every new person that they bring in, they are more likely to drive out positive hard workers and build a bad employee experience.

Unfortunately, it's not always obvious when a culture is toxic. Those managers who create terrible subcultures are usually excellent at managing up, and it can take drastic events or a significant amount of time for leaders to realize something is wrong (if they ever do).

If you are an executive leader now, there are a few ways to identify if your culture is becoming toxic. First is the tried-and-true employee survey. While individuals are unlikely to call out a toxic culture directly in their results (especially if it is a small company with limited responses), you can generally see when the engagement scores are significantly lower for a particular leader, either over an extended period of time or within a specific culture question.

Second is to open up opportunities for high-visibility projects across a few key target groups. A toxic subculture breeds psychological instability and lack of emotional safety, so employees are less likely to take on high-risk projects or to be willing to share potentially bad news with their boss.

Last is to pay keen attention to who in the leadership team is not promoting within their organization or providing their people opportunities to present to senior leadership directly. A good leader is building deep skillsets within their organization to support progression, while a toxic leader will stifle others who they feel may be competition or make them look bad.

This is why the higher you get in leadership, the harder it is to maintain a great subculture—you are no longer hiring or directly managing each individual leader. It is also why a ghost culture starts to form—the executive leads well, hires people who also lead well, but then as the management tree builds out below them it gets further and further from the original goal. Building positive subcultures below each organizational vertical should be the top priority for every leadership team to ensure higher retention levels and good job market reputation for recruiting.

Now that you're in the position to build your leadership—and ultimately company—culture, you have won the career game. It's now your turn to create an environment for more hopeful individuals to progress their own careers in kind. Like yours, their journey through career ambiguity and uncertainty, bolstered by these secrets and strategies, will require intention and direction, but with your guidance it will lead your new protégées to the success they are looking for.

CHAPTER 14
Conclusion

cor·po·rate

/kôrp(ə)rət/ adjective

relating to a corporation, especially a large company or group.

A PAWN PROMOTION IN chess, also referred to as 'queening the pawn,' is a move that allows a pawn to become any other piece on the board. Through this process the pawn, though initially a weak piece, can become the strongest player on the board through strategic moves and countermoves. This is not a play that happens accidentally—it happens through a careful strategy and understanding the clear rules of the game.

Finding your career success does not have to be a game of guesses hoping for an accidental queening. Instead, you can structure your time and efforts strategically to make the most impact in the fewest number of moves. This will allow you to progress your career quickly, while building advocates and great relationships along the way.

What it takes to make these moves successfully is not obvious in every company, but the secrets and correlating strategies of this book teach the most impactful lessons I have collected from thousands of clients. Networking, brand building, self-advocacy, and communication are vital across all industries and job types.

We can all feel isolated in our careers and put on blinders to the tactics that are helping our peers progress more quickly while facing issues and complications that feel unique to us. And while there are certainly nuances in each workplace experience, often we are living the same lives in a different font. This means that tactics that work to improve one person's situation can often help improve our own, if we get out of our own way and apply them.

This is why what happens next, after you're done reading this book, is so important. While reading this advice is step one, executing it requires intention, strategy, and the investment of your time. I highly recommend going back and completing each of the assignments (if you didn't the first time) and implementing each strategy in your workplace. Understand your unique skills, build your network, prepare for competency evaluations, develop your skills with each jump in seniority, become a great manager, and establish a great culture that helps you reach new heights in your personal career journey.

Then reference back to the list of secrets and strategies to help you navigate your workplace.

Secret #1: You are an entrepreneur, and your career is your business
Run your career like a business

Secret #2: Relationships matter more than the work
Develop your work relationships

Secret #3: Communication is key
Upskill your communication

Secret #4: No one is responsible for your career but you
Accept responsibility for your career

Secret #5: You must have and maintain healthy boundaries
Use boundaries to prioritize, bundle, and rebrand

Secret #6: Your boss does not know what you are working on

Don't keep your successes secret from your boss

Secret #7: How you talk about your work matters

Understand the three types of work

Secret #8: If you do not have an impact, you will not see progression

Maximise your impact above all else

Secret #9: An unneeded skill is unvaluable

Take your strengths where they are most needed

Secret #10: What people think of you at work is directly in your control

Keep your brand message on the tip of your tongue

Secret #11: Your brand will enter the room long before you do and leave long after you are gone

Let your brand do the heavy lifting for you

Secret #12: People prefer to work with people that they like

Make sure you know what your boss thinks about your competencies

Secret #13: A desire for a promotion without a plan will land you exactly where you are now 12 months in the future

Learn to brag

Secret #14: Work that your boss doesn't know about doesn't matter

Cover your… assets

Secret #15: Most conversations about your career will take place without you in the room

Set yourself up for cross-calibration success

Secret #16: Your potential, not your performance, is what gets you into senior leadership

Boost the soft skills that will show your potential

Secret #17: Building your leadership skills allows for not only your success but the success of your team

Develop the skills needed not only for the level you're working at, but for the levels you aspire to

Secret #18: Your network must extend beyond your own team
Grow your network organically

Secret #19: Without a network you will fail
Grow your network intentionally

Secret #20: People who help *you* will think of you more fondly than people *you* help
Allow the people in your network to help you first

Secret #21: How you communicate your disagreement is more important than your opinion
Learn the type of person you're disagreeing with

Secret #22: Catering your communication to the individual will prevent conflict and disagreements before they arise
Practice nemawashi

Secret #23: You are not always going to get your way
Accept that some of your best ideas will be rejected

Secret #24: Managing and leading are not the same
Understand the three pillars of effective management

Secret #25: Success starts at assignment, not at completion
Conduct management ceremonies

Secret #26: A successful employee begets a successful leader
Build an advocacy plan for your team

Secret #27: Negative patterns are more problematic than negative people
Manage the patterns, not the person

Secret #28: You can't compensate for your team
Build your team up with growth in mind

Secret #29: Strategy is essential
Build yourself a strategy

Secret #30: Managing your mental load should take priority over managing your workload

Choose your tactics for reducing mental load

Secret #31: A toxic workplace isn't good for anyone

Leverage your workplace support networks

Secret #32: It takes time to recover from a toxic workplace

Between jobs, give yourself time to rebuild your confidence in yourself and in your skills

Secret #33: Most people will never be executives

If you want to be an executive, prepare to leave your comfort zone behind

Secret #34: The right path for your career is a natural alignment to your skills and interests

Avoid the 'accidental career' trap

Secret #35: Only the culture of your direct manager matters

Get to the truth of your employer company's culture

Secret #36: The leaders you hire determine your company culture

Recruit great leaders

The goal of all of my content is to help people understand how they can find progression and career alignment with their passions, which is why this book touches on not just climbing to the highest seat in the house (do you even want a corner office?) but also how to understand your own skills, passions, and interests to create career synergy with your values (your most marketable skills). Success can look different across cultures, genders, marital status, residence location, and general personality—you should not feel pressured for your success to mirror that of anyone else. Instead, you need to learn yourself and be able to create a career strategy that aligns with your passions and leaves you satisfied at the end of every week. And remember: I don't want you to work more hours. Working any amount of time for the sake of appearing busy is a huge waste of effort, and working overtime rarely benefits anyone. Instead I want you to do the most valuable work, that gets you what you desire in your career, for the least amount of effort possible.

You must decide how much you are willing to work and on what. You must shift your mentality from, 'I work so hard but no one seems to notice or appreciate it' to, 'My job is to educate my leadership on the efforts required to deliver work in a way that brings value to my time.' And you must determine what boundaries you have and when (if ever) you are willing to break them for work. Only after you are prepared to create a life that fits your needs, will you be able to effectively scale the career ladder (or lattice) without sacrificing your mental health.

In the end, you have one life to optimize to the best of your ability, and as long as what you're doing is fulfilling and satisfying, then you're on the right path.

I hope that this book gives you the confidence to step into your unique strengths, values, and branding in a way that facilitates your ideal career. I hope that you wake tomorrow with a renewed sense of purpose and clarity. And finally, I hope you have heard and understood the secrets of this career game we find ourselves playing, so that every move you make works out to your advantage.

Good luck!

ACKNOWLEDGMENTS

THANK YOU TO my ride-or-die husband David, without whom none of the great opportunities that led to this book would have been possible.

Thank you to my children, K & E, who taught me there was so much more to life than just my career, while supporting me in my journey through the game regardless.

Thank you to my mother September who cheered for me when I was too afraid to cheer for myself and to my father Joe for teaching me persistence.

To Vinod, Vince, AJ, Dillon, Taylor, Bryan, Patrick, Alison, Dror, Raj, and Mike for being amazing leaders, mentors, guides, and sounding boards as I progressed through my own career.

Thank you to my editor Nick Fletcher and his ongoing support through the writing, editing, and publishing process.

To my friends Natalie, Bethany, Rachel, Leslee, and Megan your friendships and support have guided me through all my uncertainties; and to Kara who not only supported me in my journey but provided guidance and encouraged me as a fellow author.

And most of all thanks be to God who wrote my path for me and lights my steps.

ENDNOTES

1 Zenger, John H.; Folkman, Joe; and Edinger, Scott K, *The Inspiring Leader: Unlocking the Secrets of How Extraordinary Leaders Motivate*, New York: McGraw Hill, 2009.

2 Minsky, Marvin, *The Emotion Machine: Commonsense Thinking, Artificial Intelligence, and the Future of the Human Mind*, New York: Simon & Schuster, 2007.

3 Kahn, Roomy, 'Crowdsourcing Referrals: The New Holy Grail Of Hiring,' *Forbes*, December 7, 2023. Retrieved from www.forbes.com/sites/roomykhan/2023/12/07/crowdsourcing-referrals-the-new-holy-grail-of-hiring.

ABOUT THE AUTHOR

AS THE FOUNDER of That Career Coach, Kendall Berg helps her clients and followers understand how to find progression, recognition, and support in their careers. She regularly supports her more than 500,000 followers across Instagram, TikTok, and YouTube with her take on playing the career game.

Prior to starting her company, Kendall worked with and for some of the largest companies in the world, including Capital One, JP Morgan Chase, Samsung, and AT&T. In her role as a director of technology strategy with these companies she has led strategic initiatives and culture programs geared towards career progression supporting hundreds of thousands of employees. Over the course of her career, she has spoken to peer audiences of more than 1000 people and travelled the United States sharing her advice with clients and corporations alike.

Kendall's social media and podcast provide insights on corporate behind the scenes, recommendations on how to advocate for yourself and progress your career, and advice for navigating difficult interpersonal situations. She has more than 20 million views and 1.4 million likes on TikTok, 30 million views and 2 million likes on Instagram, and engages with more than 6 million accounts each month.